OBEDIENCE

A Season to Observe, Obey, & Overcome

By: Sheirra Marci, Ed.D.

KING JESUS PRESS LLC

OBEDIENCE

A SEASON TO OBSERVE, OBEY, & OVERCOME

SHEIRRA MARCI, Ed.D.

ISBN: 979-8-9939574-0-1 Softcover

ISBN: 979-8-9939574-1-8 Hardcover

ISBN: 979-8-9939574-2-5 E-book

Unless otherwise indicated, Scripture verses quoted are from the King James Version of the Bible, public domain.

Author photo courtesy of: Kimazing Photography

PRAISE FOR OBEDIENCE

"Obedience: A Season to Observe, Obey, & Overcome" is a deeply personal voyage into transparency. All too often, we forget that the journey with Christ isn't for the weak or fearful, but for the obedient and faithful. In seven compelling chapters, Dr. Sheirra Marci reflectively opens up about her genuine journey of faith; filled with lessons learned, losses faced, and the constant grace that has seen her through every challenge.

This third installment in her spiritual series tackles real-life issues head-on: from the pain of disobedience, the burden of consequences, and the bravery it takes to let go when God whispers for us to take a path that doesn't quite seem clear. Yet throughout, there's a thread of redemption and resilience woven into every lesson and constant reminder that even when we stumble or fall, God's mercy is always there to catch us.

Dr. Sheirra Marci not only shares her experiences of fear, hesitation, and uncertainty, but she emphasizes that obedience to God isn't about perfection; it's about trust. Her openness offers peace and comfort to anyone who's struggled to follow God's guidance, anyone who aspires to reconnect, and anyone who simply needs a reminder that God never fails.

Simply put, "**Obedience: A Season to Observe, Obey, & Overcome**" goes beyond just *her* story it's a call for you to reflect on your own journey with God, learn from your trials, and find joy in overcoming with Him every step of the way.

My grandmother used to always say, "I don't know what tomorrow holds, but I know who holds my tomorrow;" consider this book a written confirmation that the prayers of those before you, are still powering the grace of God within you in every season of your life.

Chantay Williams, Music Producer/Curator

DEDICATION

To Alijah, you will always be my reason why. You are the reason why I share my experiences with others so it can inspire and uplift them. You are the reason I work tirelessly to be the best version of me. Never forget, God has equipped you with everything you need to be successful. Use the gifts He has provided. I love you!

To Mother, Momma K, and Daddy, I did it again! Thank you all for being supportive and loving me unconditionally. I am so grateful to have you in my life. I love you all very much.

To my late grandparents, I miss you all so much. Continue to rest well. Until we meet again, I love you all. You all are forever in my heart.

To my siblings, Sergio, Pachess, Shaundra, Amanda, Scott Jr., thank you so much for your authentic support. I love you all.

To my nieces and nephews, Katura, Sumarra, Scott III, Serenity, and Samson, I love you all. I am very grateful for the moments I get to share with each of you.

Remember, you can do anything you set your heart and mind to do if you just try.

To all my aunties, uncles, and cousins, your love and support mean everything to me. I love you all.

To Auntie Barbara, I love you and miss you so much. I appreciate the love and support that you always showed me while you were here with me. You will never be forgotten. Until we meet again, rest well.

To Angela McCrory, our blood made us cousins, but you were so much more. There were times when you were a 3rd mom to me and a 3rd grandmother to Alijah. For that I am forever grateful. You did so much for me in this lifetime that there are not enough words to convey the appreciation and love that I have for you. Forever in my heart, until we meet again, rest well.

To Richard Moss, you will live on in our hearts. You will not be forgotten.

To my Sista Circle, the SIS Organization, close friends, and best friends, thank you for being honest and authentic. Your support means the world to me. I love you all.

To anyone reading this book, this book is for you! May it bless, inspire, encourage and uplift you during your journey through life. One thing I have learned on my journey through life is that obedience is better than sacrifice. Always remember that God is able to do exceedingly abundantly above all that we could ask or think. Never give up! Keep the faith! Trust God! Obey His word!

CONTENTS

FOREWORD

Obedience is one of the greatest tests of faith - a journey that stretches the heart, challenges the mind, and refines the soul. In *Obedience: A Season to Observe, Obey, & Overcome*, Dr. Sheirra Marci invites readers into a deeply personal exploration of what it truly means to trust God through every storm, setback, and season of silence.

With raw transparency, she shares her own encounters with grief and disobedience – the moments when life felt heavy, and following God's direction seemed harder than expected. She does not hide the weight of her battles, nor does she shy away from the lessons that came through tears and trial. Instead, she courageously exposes what many ignore: how disobedience often stems from pain, how grief can cloud judgment, and how easily life's experiences can pull us off course when our emotions lead instead of our faith.

What makes this book so impactful is how the author breaks down each test, one by one, drawing readers closer to understanding themselves and God's process. She shows that every trial carries a teaching, every delay holds direction, and every disappointment conceals divine development. Through her words, we learn that obedience is not about being unshaken – it is about learning to remain *calm, self-controlled, and steadfast* even when everything around us feels uncertain.

This book is both a mirror and a map – a reflection of our own struggles and a guide through the process of overcoming them. It challenges readers to face battles head-on rather than run from them, revealing that victory often lies on the other side of surrender.

May these pages remind you that obedience is not a punishment, but a path – one that leads from brokenness to breakthrough, from hesitation to healing, and from struggle to strength.

Prophetess Brandi M. Echols

INTRODUCTION

Obedience is defined as complying to a request, order or law. When we comply with things, we act in accordance with a command or abide by a rule. Another way we define obedience is submitting to authority, such as our parents. When we are obedient to our parents, it means we abide by explicit instructions without deviating. Most of us know, if we were disobedient children, there were consequences. From a spiritual perspective, obedience means listening to God and doing what He asks us to do. When I think of my own personal experiences, I can admit I have learned some tough lessons. One of my favorite phrases is, "Obedience is better than sacrifice." Yet even as an adult, I find myself not listening to what God tells me to do. As a result, I endure unnecessary consequences.

In the third installment of my book series, "Obedience: A Season to Observe, Obey, & Overcome," I am once again open and authentic about my relationship with God, the consequences I encountered being disobedient, and my season of overcoming. This book is divided into seven chapters which include: Spiritual Test II, Observation Test, Obedience Test, Obstacles Test,

Obstacles Test II, Grief Test, and Overcoming Test. I selected these chapters to convey the consequences I faced when I was disobedient to God's word, despite having a strong relationship with Him.

Spiritual Test II is the first chapter. It is labeled as a second installment because my first book, "Perseverance: A Reflection of Pain, Passion, and Purpose," contains a Spiritual Test chapter also. In this Spiritual Test II chapter, I am very candid as I discuss how God asked me to do different things at two different times in my life, and I was disobedient. It provides a vivid picture of how my relationship with God is still evolving today. Even though I endured some tough consequences for being disobedient, God was still faithful through it all. He provided grace and mercy during my disobedience. I share several experiences I encountered over the years and how God brought me through. In addition, I explain how being obedient served me well.

In the Observation Test chapter, I discuss how important it is to take a moment to sit back and observe what God is trying to show us. There were a few instances where I missed God's initial message because I did not open my eyes and watch clearly the things that were right in front of me. As a result, I was wrongly released from a job with a natural gas provider (GS) after 10 years of service and needed to make some tough decisions. Sometimes all God wants us to do is watch and pray. There is joy is just observing.

In the Obedience Test chapter, I touch on two instances where God told me to resign from two jobs, but I did not leave because I thought I needed the income. Due to my disobedience, I was released from both jobs involuntarily. God is good at reminding me that He is in control and when he tells me to do something, He expects me to do it. In addition to being told to leave two jobs, God told me to launch an organization two years before I actually did it. Fear, as outlined in this chapter, caused me to be disobedient in these instances.

In the Obstacles Test chapter, I express how I had to navigate several obstacles that came my way in such a short time. It seemed there was something happening back-to-back. I was overwhelmed. I was scared. I was hurt. I was angry. I was upset. This chapter allows me to explain just how scary obstacles can be and how God was with me through it all.

In the Obstacles Test II chapter, I discuss my transparent experience with looking for a job as a highly educated Black woman and coming up short more often than not. I discuss honest details that led me to capitalize on resources I did not know were available to me. However, as a dislocated worker, classified exclusively by the Georgia Department of Labor, it created an opportunity that would continue to help build and boost my résumé. I briefly discuss my new job opportunity and what it took to obtain this blessing. It was a reminder that God is faithful through it all.

In the Grief Test chapter, I am vulnerable and honest about my fight with grief. Over the last decade I have encountered numerous losses in my family that have caused me to question many things. There were times when I wanted to cry, but I could not cry. There were times when I felt like screaming, but I could not scream. Grief is an overwhelming feeling that everyone processes differently. I understood there was not a one size fits all for the grieving process. However, I knew to protect my mental space, it was necessary to do something. In this chapter I was candid about the steps I took after experiencing numerous deaths back-to-back. It allowed me to re-evaluate things in my life to ensure I handled these occurrences adequately. The truth is loss is hard. Therefore, grief is a major part of this process. It was essential for me to learn how to manage these things when they occurred.

Finally, in the Overcoming Test chapter, I explain just how I overcame a tough time in my life, despite the obstacles. Initially, I did not know how I would get through the situations I was going through. However, I reminded myself that God would make a way even when I could not see a way. I realized that even in my disobedience, God was with me. He looked out for me. He protected me. He blessed me despite the decisions I made, good or bad. Dive in and take another walk with me as I share candid and real experiences on my obedience journey!

Chapter 1
SPIRITUAL TEST: PART II

My spiritual relationship with Jesus is constantly evolving. I have learned more about myself from a spiritual perspective that I did not know years ago. Some of those things consist of being vulnerable and knowing when to cry out to Him for direction. At times, vulnerability is labeled as being weak, but I feel it is a strength we should all practice. In my weakest moments, I draw strength from my Heavenly Father. I have also learned when to be still and listen to His words. I am constantly moving. Between tutoring my students, running small businesses, supporting other obligations, and being a mom, partner, daughter, and so much more, there is rarely a moment where I am not doing something. Therefore, being intentional about hearing from Him is something I have learned to do more. Finally, I have enhanced the way I pray. There were times in my prayer life that I did not know what to say or where to start. Often when I prayed, I expressed what was in my heart. Since He knows my heart, I was confident in knowing that if I missed something or someone, He knew my heart. There are still times when I do not have the words to say, so I seek him more for the right words.

Throughout my spiritual relationship with Jesus, the journey has not been easy. It has been enlightening, scary, overwhelming, rewarding and challenging. Yet, I am grateful for the opportunity to grow in Christ at this point in my life. It is very necessary. Each year He blesses me with, I am committed to giving him more of my time, praise and honor. He is truly worthy!

As a PGK (preacher's grandkid) I was raised in the church. I went to church a lot and was held to higher standards than others. When I moved in with my father in 1994, attending church was something I had to do. I did not have a choice. Whether it was Tuesday or Wednesday for prayer, Thursday or Friday for Bible Study, Sunday morning, and Sunday night, I had to be there. Not to mention in January, we attended church every weeknight for one hour. In addition, there were months when we had revivals, conventions, convocations, and our youth program that required us to attend church Monday-Friday, with the official conclusion on Sunday morning and/or Sunday night. It was a lot to handle and often overwhelming as a child. However, it shaped my spiritual relationship with Jesus.

Attending church was just that, attending services in a physical building. Many of us at some point in our lives just attended church. Not only was attending church something I did when I moved in with my father, it was something I did with my mother as well. As a little girl, my mother took my sister and me to church. Our frequency was only on Sundays, but she made sure we went. In addition, my late Grandma Perkins provided several opportunities to attend church as well. Essentially, there was no way to avoid going to church.

Frankly, I never had a problem going to church. I truly enjoyed being in the building praising and worshipping Jesus. The spirit was always moving when I was at church, which sparked my curiosity. Being in the presence of Jesus was an amazing feeling. However, I did not learn until much later in life that I can be in the presence of Jesus anywhere. Even though attending church was a good start, I learned that building a relationship with Jesus was something I had to do for myself. This went beyond just attending church. I had a desire to establish a meaningful relationship with Him. I could no longer rely on my family to create that relationship for me.

Whether it was voluntary or involuntary, I was always in church. Though most of my childhood I attended church, there was a brief period in my life when I did not go. Many would say, I was going through a period of rebellion, but I was hurting. The most effective way for me to deal with the hurt was to stay home. This meant I did not attend church for several weeks.

When I was coerced into getting married because I got pregnant with my son, I agreed because my late Grandmother Dean told me it was the best thing to do. By getting married, it meant I would not have to stand in front of the entire congregation to apologize for getting pregnant out of wedlock – or so I thought. In addition, it meant I would not have to resign from the positions I held in the church. Yet, I was told by my grandmother or father – I do not recall which one – if I did not attend church to apologize, according to my grandfather, there would be severe consequences. I did not understand why I had to do this. The request was humiliating and unfair. As a result, afterwards I did not attend church for several weeks.

Many would say this is an example of "church hurt" or convince themselves what they would not do. We can easily say what we would or would not do, until we are in that position. Then when we are faced with these same challenges, things change. I was still very young during that time. I was very conscious of the things I did or said because I felt it impacted my family. I was in that space of trying to do things to please my family. I had a fear of disappointing them. Unfortunately, that was such a tough lesson for me to learn. It took a very long time for me to get to a place where I was not solely concerned with how my family felt about the decisions I made. I quickly realized that only Jesus could judge me, and He would do so accordingly.

After I spent several weeks away from church I did go back. I was missing a key element of my life. I know most people would have stayed away longer or never went back, but my purpose was so much bigger than my hurt. Going to church, praising my Heavenly Father, being involved in different roles (choir member, usher, and secretary) reading His word, and supporting the work were all things I authentically wanted to do. Often as a child I heard the older saints saying, "Let the LORD use you." Initially, I did not know what that meant, but the sound of Jesus using me sparked my curiosity all over again. I liked the sound of Him using me. Despite the things I went through, I was still willing to attend church and serve Him. I did not allow the hurt I endured to keep me away from all the blessings He had in store for me.

Throughout my spiritual journey, I had some tough lessons to learn. Some lessons I learned quickly. Other lessons took longer to learn and some I am still learning. No matter how long it takes, I am committed to learning. Fear has been a constant struggle on my walk with Christ. It is a lesson I am still learning. One of my favorite Scriptures comes from II Timothy 1:7 King James Version (KJV) which states, "For God hath not given us the spirit of fear; but of power, and of love, and of a sound mind." My interpretation of this Scripture is God did not give us the spirit to worry, fret or fear which means if we truly trust in Him, fear should not exist. It is so easy to say we are not afraid of things, but in those moments when we should step out on faith, we hesitate, or we do not do it at all.

In 2008, after years of struggling to maintain a stable home for my son, I decided no matter what it took, I would ensure we always had a stable place to call home. Since I had this mindset, I worked several jobs at a time to generate income. When I left high school in June of 1999, I had my first job in retail management the following month. I was grateful for the church member

6

who referred me to her manager. God was already working things out for me, and I was grateful. As a result of the referral and a great interview, I was hired. Retail management was not the ideal career path for me, but I was good at it, and it paid most of the bills.

I started at Cato and moved around to several big retailers which included Macy's Staples, Ross and Macy's. Prior to 2013, the only credentials I had was my high school diploma. I did not know how to negotiate salaries. I accepted what my employers offered because something was better than nothing at all. After concluding my time with Cato in 2004, I started my journey at Ross. I attended a job fair for the North Dekalb Mall location in Decatur, Georgia, but the store manager at the Stonecrest, Georgia location handpicked me for her store. She told me I did so well during the interview process that she wanted to hire me for her store. I was excited and learned a lot during my time with her. After several years at that location, I put in a transfer request to the location in East Point. I was also working at Target in East Point, so it was easier to get to Ross in the same shopping center. My transfer request was approved, and I started my journey at the new Ross location.

Things at the East Point location was very hectic and stressful. Whenever the corporate executives were in town, they always visited our store because it was the last one before going to the airport. This meant we had to prepare for visits often, which required an empty stock room and high-level recovery of the store. It was challenging, but we got it done. After moving to Cobb County in 2005, it was important for me to be close to home. With the help of one of the area supervisors at the Cumberland location in Smyrna, Georgia I was approved for another transfer. I was grateful for the change, but it was not better. I became the front-end supervisor for this location, which resulted in more responsibilities. I handled things well and performed in my role. However, the store management team lacked the key skills necessary to perform in their role. The management team changed frequently because the district management team was trying to find the best fit for the store. No matter what changes were made, the store struggled. This made things challenging for the back-up supervisors, which included my role as the front-end supervisor.

In addition to my role, I was the lead cash office specialist. This meant I trained all managers and new associates who needed to be trained in this role. God knew it was too much, but I knew it was a solid income. After several changes in store managers, we finally received a new store manager who came from the Ross location in Cartersville. We were hopeful that we would finally have stability, but that was not the case. Our new manager was strictly by the rule book. It was her way, or you no longer had a job. She had a problem each time the area managers expressed their concerns regarding the store. She was not receptive to feedback or any suggestions. She had her own way of running the store and our recommendations did not matter. It was such a difficult position to be in. Whenever possible, I kept a safe distance. She did not like how I was very vocal regarding things that needed to improve. She felt I was outspoken as I constantly expressed my dissatisfaction with how the store was being run. It was a lot to deal with, but I was doing the best I could.

One afternoon while working at the register, I started having sharp pains in my chest. It was something I had never experienced before. Thankfully, we had chairs upfront for our senior customers who needed to rest while their loved ones shopped. It allowed me to sit down for a little bit to determine if the pain would subside. It did not. After a few short minutes passed, the manager on duty decided it was necessary to call the ambulance. When the ambulance arrived, I remembered them checking my vitals and suggesting I go to the emergency room since my complaint was chest pains.

When I arrived, the medical team ran several tests, scans, and drew blood. After several hours, the doctor shared with me the chest pains were a result of an anxiety attack. An anxiety attack? "What is that?" wondered. I did not have to think about it too long because the doctor informed me of the leading cause of an anxiety attack. Stress. Of course, the preliminary diagnosis led to a series of other questions from the doctor that were overwhelming. I never realized work was impacting my health in this way. This was the final sign from God that it was time to go. At that point I had worked for Ross for almost nine years, making less than $10 an hour, and it was now negatively impacting my health. It was not worth it. What was I going to do? I needed the income and though the income was very minimal, it was consistent.

After speaking with the doctor and hearing the options, I declined the prescription for anxiety medication. Even though I felt I did not need medication, I knew some changes needed to be made. The doctor provided follow up care instructions and discharged me from the emergency room. I was thankful I did not have to stay overnight. When I got home, I knew I had some tough decisions to make. Sadly, I did not know where to start. Ross provided a solid income, but it was stressful, unorganized, hectic, and negatively impacting my health.

After the anxiety attack at work, I remained at Ross for a little while longer. Often, we hold on to things and people that God is trying to tear us away from. We feel comfortable. We feel secure, but we are afraid. The fear of the unknown keeps us from taking the leap that God wants us to take. After the anxiety episode, there was no way I should have remained at Ross, but I did. When you are a child of God, there is high level of expectations. As the Bible tells us in Luke 12:48 (KJV), "But he that knew not, and did commit things worthy of stripes, shall be beaten with few stipes. For unto whomsoever much is given, of him shall be much required: and to whom men have committed much, of him they will ask the more."

This means that individuals who may not know the word of God will have more leniency than those who know the word and do not obey. God requires more from His children, and since I know I am a child of the Most High, I realized my expectations are greater. The fear of not having adequate income kept me at Ross until I had no choice but leave.

One night after the store closed for the night, the closing team was on the sales floor recovering. Since the front-end of the store was my responsibility, I made sure it was cleaned and organized when I closed. I had a purchase to make so I asked one of the cashiers to ring me up. Once the transaction was completed, we wrapped up our recovery efforts and left for the night. Maybe a week later, I was called to the office while ringing up customers. It was not uncommon to be called to the office at any time, but it was weird to be called to the office during a time that was very busy. When I walked into the office, the atmosphere did not feel right. The store manager, assistant store manager, and the loss prevention manager were all talking but immediately stopped when I walked in. What was going on? When did the loss prevention manager arrive? The loss prevention manager did all the talking. The store manager and assistant store manager seemed to only be present as witnesses. The knots in my stomach were intense. The feeling I felt in that moment was fear because I did not know what was going on.

The loss prevention manager asked if I knew why I was called into the office. My response was no. She shared with me that I made a purchase while on company time, and it was a violation of company's policy. I stared at her because she could not be serious. Before I knew it, I asked, "When did this become a violation of company's policy when many employees, including managers, make purchases on their 15-minute break or, most commonly, at the end of the night when the store is closed?"

She shared with me it was always a policy according to the employee handbook. She asked me to write a statement explaining how I felt about the accusations. Once my statement was written, she reviewed it and told me she had to release me from my role as front-end supervisor. Was she serious? With disgust, I got up and walked out of the office. The assistant store manager walked with me because she had to escort me out of the store. She told me to keep my head up. When I was outside of the store, I breathed a sigh of relief. A calmness came over me that I had not felt before. I got in my car and drove home.

When I got home, I realized I no longer had a job or consistent income. For the first time since I was released from Ross, fear settled in. After almost nine years of service, I was released from a company for such a bogus reason. I was filled with several different emotions at the same time. I was angry. I was hurt. I felt undervalued. I was worried about how I would pay my bills without a job or income. Then I was reminded, "God will never leave me nor forsake me." The calmness I felt walking out of Ross came over me again. It was at that moment I knew everything would be alright. In addition to working full-time at Ross, I was also a full-time student. I was at the end of my associate's program and determined to finish, so I knew I needed to remain focused despite the current situation.

Shortly after being released from my job, I talked to one of my close friends who I met while working for Ross. I told her what happened, and she could not believe it. She felt the reason they let me go was bogus, and she encouraged me to apply for unemployment. Due to previous failed attempts, I had no intention of filing for unemployment. It seemed every time I had applied for it, they quickly denied me. I just did not want to waste time going through the process to obtain the same results. My friend was persistent. She encouraged me to apply regardless because this time could be different. After some thought, I decided to apply. I knew the worst that could happen was receiving another "no." I went into the Department of Labor Service Center, and they assisted me with filing a claim. It was such a tedious process, but I got it done.

In the meantime, I decided to apply for a new job. One of the requirements to receive unemployment payments was to be actively looking for work. In addition to actively seeking work, I had to be available for any job offers I received. I had a solid game plan. I knew I needed a job to pay my bills. I updated my resume and applied for multiple jobs. I attended job fairs. I emailed my resume to different employers. I signed up for staffing agencies and I applied for more jobs. Trying to find a job was a job. Within just a few short days, I had job offers with Good Will and Alorica. It was hard deciding which job I should take. One job wanted me to start orientation on the same day I was scheduled to graduate from college. "Could I really miss walking with my classmates due to a new job?" I worked hard to get to this point. Missing graduation was not an option. However, I needed a job. I was torn.

One afternoon when I returned home from running errands, I stopped by the mailbox. There was a letter from the Department of Labor. I was not thinking much about the contents of the letter, so I waited until I got in the house to open it. When I opened the letter, it told me that as a recipient of unemployment, I had to attend workshops at the local Department of Labor Service Center. At that moment, I was confused. I had not received any previous correspondence from the Department of Labor. In addition, I had not received any payments. Or maybe I received a payment, but I did not know. After reading the letter several times, the Spirit led me to check my bank account. I wondered if it was typical for the unemployment office to issue payments without notifying individuals they were approved.

To my surprise when I logged into my bank account, there were deposits from the Department of Labor for unemployment benefits. It was at least three weeks of payments which covered the previous weeks I claimed benefits. I was overwhelmed with emotions and thanked God for this blessing. After a few denials, I was finally approved for unemployment. God was truly worthy of the honor and praise in that moment. The next day I officially received the approval letter. It included the weekly amount and the length of time I would receive benefits. Based on this information and the emergency tiers I was eligible for, I decided to not take any new job offers and just focus on school.

Receiving unemployment benefits gave me the flexibility to spend more time with family and do things I was not able to do while working for an employer. I put Alijah in football and was an active part of his football journey. God was already working things out for me, and I did not realize it. There is a saying that I live by: "God will make a way, even when we cannot see a way." God is so faithful through it all. Through the good, bad, happy, sad, and complicated times, He is always right on time. God does not always come when we want Him to, but He is always on time. In addition to receiving unemployment benefits, I started my tutoring business which allowed me to generate additional income as well. God showed me He would take care of me if I just trust in Hand obey His word. I was so grateful.

For 14 months, I received unemployment benefits. I remember Congress blocking the extension of unemployment benefits in December 2013, which resulted in no additional tiers being granted. Therefore, in May 2014 my unemployment benefits were coming to an end. Even though I was still tutoring kids, the sessions were not as consistent as I needed them to be. I knew I had to return to work to ensure I generated the income necessary to handle my monthly obligations. Since retail management was a job I held since I graduated from high school, it was only common for me to seek jobs in retail. It was a profession I knew I was good at. Not long after I started applying for new jobs, I received a job offer from CVS. I was hired on the spot at a job fair and returned to work shortly after. It was not long after I started working for CVS that I was filled with regret. The store manager who hired me at the job fair turned out to be a person who was very difficult to work for. He lacked the ability to talk to employees with compassion and respect. He talked down to us. As I was preparing for work one morning, God reminded me, "I delivered you from retail for a reason." I had to stop for a moment and acknowledge that being released from Ross was not a loss but a gain. It was the profession where I was most comfortable.

God had so much more in store for me. Retail management was not the end of my story. However, I could not adequately accept my assignment if I did not fully lean and depend on God. After a few short months of being employed with CVS, I was convinced I would waste another nine years with a company that did not value me as an employee. I started applying for other opportunities. I used staffing agencies to find work in other industries. I was in desperate need of a change.

OBEDIENCE

My shift at CVS was perfect. It was the only thing I enjoyed about working for the company. I worked Monday-Thursday from 6 a.m. – 2 p.m. Thankfully, the schedule for the following week was always posted on Thursdays since that was the last day I worked each week. One Thursday, when I clocked out for the day, I checked the schedule to determine when I returned to work. I was on the schedule from Monday-Thursday like normal. When I attempted to clock in on Monday, the system indicated I needed an override because I was not scheduled. I was puzzled. Typically, when there is a schedule change, managers are supposed to notify employees. However, that was not the case. Since I could not clock in without needing an override, I walked to the back to review my schedule. To my surprise, I was no longer on the schedule. All my scheduled days were gone.

I politely asked the store manager if I was supposed to work. He yelled at me like I was a child and told me to read my schedule. I shared with the manager that I was no longer on the schedule and asked if he wanted me to stay. Again, he was very rude and yelled at me to clock in. Baffled by his behavior, I clocked in, got his approval, and started my day. When my shift was over, I clocked out and went home. There was no explanation of why I had a full schedule one day and was completely removed from the schedule the next. The behavior of the store manager was unprofessional, and I was ready to cut ties with CVS.

God was, once again, working on my behalf. The next day Hire Dynamics called to let me know GS was interested in interviewing me for their customer service position. This role was a change, and I needed a change. I did very well during my interview and received positive feedback from both the leaders at GS and Hire Dynamics. Unfortunately, I received a call from Hire Dynamics letting me know GS selected 10 candidates, and I was number 11. Although I was a little sad, I knew God was in complete control. The rep from Hire Dynamics let me she would give me call if anything changed.

The next day I received another call from Hire Dynamics letting me know that GS did want to hire me for the customer care position. I was so excited and ready for the fresh start. Ironically, the same day CVS called to let me know the manager placed me back on the schedule Monday-Thursday of the following week. I shared with the supervisor that I would be coming into the store that same day to bring my resignation letter. I told her my resignation would be effective immediately. She was shocked but understood. I told her it was important that they found someone else to work my schedule, because I would not be there. When I arrived at the store to turn in my letter of resignation, the supervisor shared with me the manager was not happy. I shared with her until he learns how to treat his employees, he will continue to lose good, quality individuals. I gave her my letter and walked out of the store.

I thanked God for delivering me from retail once again. I was convinced my days in retail were over. I would no longer use retail as a source of income just because it was my comfort zone. I knew I was so much greater than retail and I needed to break away from the fear. I knew God was not done working on me, and I was preparing for what was to come.

CHAPTER 1 LESSON

Many times, God tries to pull us out of our comfort zones, but we allow fear to keep us from tapping into the greater He has for us. God already knows the potential, talents, skills and passions we possess. It is up to each of us to listen to His word and act accordingly. If He leads you in a direction, do not fight it. Pray about it. Please understand that if He brings you to it, He will bring you through it. Remember, He will never leave us nor forsake us. We must keep the faith and trust Him. Never forget that God will make a way, even when we cannot see a way.

Chapter 2
OBSERVATION TEST

Sometimes the most adequate way for us to be obedient is to observe the things and people around us. With the hustle and bustle of life, it is easy to miss or overlook the things that are right in front of us. It is important to observe the things God wants us to see. Sadly, we are often too busy to notice what He is trying to show us, and we miss the lessons or blessings. The Oxford Dictionary defines observation as "the process or act of observing something or someone carefully to gain information." If God wants us to observe someone or something and we miss the assignment, we can lose out on a vital message He has for us.

As an individual who is constantly evolving in my relationship with God, I can admit I have missed some vital messages from Him. In some cases, it resulted in serious consequences. In others, God was merciful. I often wonder what I can do to adequately observe things and people deeply the first time. What can I do to ensure I am intentional about observing things effectively without suffering a loss? How do I stop to see what God is trying to show me? God has opened my eyes to different things, but I am still observing. I am still learning. Unfortunately, it took me enduring another loss to open my eyes and truly see what God had for me.

I started working for GS, a natural gas provider, in August 2014. Like retail, my growth was delayed and often denied in my new role. Obtaining the job with GS was the financial breakthrough I knew I needed. I was able to do so much more in such a short time. I was so grateful. By January 2015, I moved my son and me into a three-bedroom, three-bathroom townhome and purchased a new car. Things were going well. I was adjusting to my new role and familiarizing myself with the rules, policies and processes. My shift with GS was perfect. I worked 7 a.m. - 4 p.m. It allowed me to get off work in time to do things for my son or tutor my students. It created the flexibility I needed to spend time with my family. Initially, I had the perfect work-life balance. For many years, I considered GS a top place to work. For the most part, they treated the employees fairly. There were many perks and incentives we were eligible for. We had an annual bonus which included a lump sum amount and a pay raise. We had Family & Fun Day events that were 100 percent covered by the company. The medical and dental insurance were feasible as well. I felt like I was winning with a company that valued the employees.

Things seemed too good to be true, but things remained good for a while. From 2014-2017 things seemed to go well. In 2017, when I decided to apply for different opportunities, that is when I was met with several NOs. Every position I applied for, I was told no. It did not matter that I was qualified and could perform the job. It was always no. When I started with GS in 2014, I made it known I was interested in training. Training was a form of teaching and because that was my passion, I knew it was the best alternative. I became a bit discouraged when I applied for different roles but was not selected.

My eyes were starting to open, but I was still blinded by the incentives they offered. I was oblivious to the politics of the corporate world. I was unaware leaders had their favorites. I did not realize at the time that positions were posted even though the leaders already knew who would fill the roles. I learned quickly that keeping to myself was frowned upon. I learned that no matter how well I performed and came to work on time, it meant absolutely nothing when it came to promotions. It was evident GS had an inability to let things go. If you behaved in a way that was unacceptable to leadership, you heard about it on every review and every interview recap session for several years. Mid-year and annual reviews were used to recap things that happened months prior instead of discussing the true essence of employees' performances.

GS was a female dominant workforce, especially in the care center. It was no surprise that women were messy and stirring up trouble even in the workplace. The sad part is it was a constant battle. I went to work every day and kept to myself. I trusted no one. It was hard to. I did not know if being friends with someone would lead to chaos or calmness. It was always uncertainty. In addition to being a female dominant workforce, the turnover rate was pretty high. This included managers and agents. Like most jobs it was hard to keep quality employees. After applying for over 20+ jobs in five years, I was mentally checking out of my role with GS. I could not believe the leaders would not allow me to use my full potential and help improve the training department. They held everything they could against me and kept me in an entry level role as long as they could. In 2019, the company experienced a reorganization which created new roles and opportunities for employees to grow within the care department.

It was not enough, but it was a good start. One of the new roles created was the specialist role. This was the highest role in the care center and only had six positions available. Individuals who were already in that position had to reapply to be considered a specialist. It was such a nerve-racking process. I remember applying for three positions, going through several interviews wondering if I would be offered a position. After a few days, I received a call from one of the hiring managers. She was calling to offer me the specialist role. I could not believe it. In the five years with the company, there was finally a manager who gave me a YES! I was so thankful. I could not express my appreciation enough.

I was grateful someone was finally willing to give me a chance to show what I could do. I excelled in my role. I caught on quickly to my new responsibilities and was able to train new specialists joining the team. Even in the new role, I kept to myself because it was hard to trust anyone. I had good reasons. There were several times I mentioned something to a teammate in confidence that got back to leadership. It caused me to shut down and stay to myself. I had a few mentors that I felt comfortable talking to. However, I found myself being guarded with them as well. My manager and I had a good relationship. We had our disagreements from time to time, but she always looked out for me. She always defended me. She always let the leaders know the impact I made on the team or the progress I made. She always encouraged me. She had tough conversations with me to help me improve in areas where I needed help. I valued her feedback. I believe she had my best interest at heart. When she was removed as the manager of our team, I was devastated. I thought to myself, if it was not broken, why fix it? With her leaving our team, there was only one other person on the team who I talked to and trusted. When she was diagnosed with cancer and had to take leave for her cancer treatments, I was all alone, and I isolated myself all over again.

I knew changes were inevitable. I just was not expecting this change. The new manager over our team was a prior specialist. I was excited because I felt she understood what we went through as specialists and would be an asset as our new manager. Unfortunately, I was so wrong. It was not a good match at all. Even though she excelled as an agent and specialist, she was not an effective manager. She did not know how to adequately address our team verbally. She talked to us like we were children. There was more division than unity on our team. We had a bad reputation because we were all women of color. It was another hectic work environment.

Thankfully in 2020, we worked remotely due to the COVID-19 pandemic, so we were no longer commuting to the office. I was grateful for the small miracle of not having to engage with my manager in person. For the next two years, we worked exclusively from home. All our meetings or engagement activities were done via Microsoft Teams. As we prepared to update our -computer information system platform, there were talks about us returning to the office to work. Our chief operating officer had already given the care center the green light to work exclusively from home permanently. However, our manager felt it was necessary for our team to commute to the office once a week because the managers were required to do so. Since our team was considered leaders, she thought we should commute to work. I did not like it, but I did it.

On August 1 2022, the teammate that I was close to and cling to the most passed away from cancer. I was heartbroken and sad. She was one of the few employees who was already with the company when I was hired. She was patient, caring, understanding, kind and authentic. It was tough dealing with her death. The thing that made matters worse was the family did not provide us with an opportunity to say our final good-byes. It was such a difficult time for me. My eyes were opening slowly but surely. I felt like God was removing everyone from my circle who I found comfort or trust in. I no longer had a manager I trusted. Neither did I have a teammate that I truly trusted. I was cordial with all my teammates. There were just one or two who I could talk to.

One of those individuals passed away unexpectedly on August 28, 2022. It was such a sad time for our team. We had recently lost one teammate, and before the month was over, we lost another one. We were all devastated. I did not have adequate time to grieve the first death before we were grieving another one. To learn our teammate was home alone with her dog when she experienced a severe asthma attack that claimed her life was heart shattering. I cried and questioned God for days because it was difficult to grasp how a person who was so loved was alone during her final hours. Even now, it breaks my heart.

Our team went through a lot of ups and downs, management changes, and deaths. Not to mention when we lost team members, we had to find new candidates to fill those positions. We had some calm after the storm, but the storm kept growing. Later that year, we found out our manager was pregnant. Though it was such an exciting time for her, it was a challenging time for us. The pregnancy made her mean and difficult to get along with. We extended grace as a team because we understood hormones are out of control during pregnancy. However, things got worse before they got better. My manager made several changes on our team without explanation. She even accused us of being lazy and not doing our job. She said all we do as a team is clock in, take calls, and go home. Those accusations were far from the truth, but it was her word against ours. By January 2023, we received notice that everyone would rotate all shifts. This was a big problem for me since I had other obligations outside of the company. As an individual who performed well, one of the incentives for high performers was being able to select preferred shifts. Working early mornings was my preference because of the things I needed to do outside of GS. Performance no longer mattered and that bothered me.

This is when the tension between the manager and me intensified. This is also when God made things uncomfortable in my current role. Prior to 2023, there were at least two instances where I started applying for jobs outside the company because I had enough. Each time God told me to be still. As anxious as I was to break free from my job, I knew how important it was to be obedient. Shortly after applying for a job outside the company and being told to be still, I received the first and only promotion from GS. I was grateful that I was obedient, and as a result, I received a well-deserved promotion.

Sadly, 2019 was the last time I heard God tell me to be still. I had no success getting into the training department after applying for a position that I was the best candidate for. Being told no again really sealed the deal for me. I mentally checked out of my role. I was convinced the manager over training was intimidated by my knowledge and education and blocked every opportunity for me to join the team. My direct manager was doing whatever she could to make work challenging for us and it was working. We bumped heads every other day. The communication between us was always hostile.

She was untrustworthy and I realized just how devious she was when I was sitting in a meeting with the Human Resources Department (HR) regarding my future with the company. It was unbelievable how she painted a picture of me as a disrespectful, aggressive, and insubordinate employee, when all I needed her to consider was the inconvenient changes to the schedule. She wrongly accused me of doing things I was not doing. She refused to work with me, and she made it clear that I was on my own. After the long meeting with HR, they advised me to prepare a statement, and we would meet again the next day. The next few days came and went and there was no meeting with HR. I waited impatiently to determine what that status of my role would be. In the meantime, I decided I would no longer be beefing with my manager. I would limit my communication with her and when it was necessary, I would do so in a way that was professional, respectful and clear. Months passed and I never had a follow up with HR.

In July 2023 our manager was terminated. She shared with us she resigned, but we learned shortly after she was let go involuntarily. She left several warnings for us to be careful, do our work, and do not trust the HR team. She made sure she left us on high alert. Based on what she told us, our jobs were in jeopardy. It was just too much. Immediately upon her departure we were assigned a new manager. This individual was not new to the specialist team but left the team several years prior.

Though this person portrayed a sweet and kind persona, it was not authentic. The new manager meant well, but she was not an adequate fit for the role. She was clueless to what it meant to be a manager over the specialist team. It was alarming how she could no longer perform the tasks as a specialist. We knew it would be a long journey ahead.

In August 2023, the new manager went over mid-year reviews with our team. I was shocked when I discovered my review included a final warning – something I never received previously. After assessing the content of the review, I respectfully declined to sign because it was not accurate. I shared with the manager what happened. I told her the second meeting that was supposed to take place back in April with HR did not happen. Therefore, a final warning should not be listed on my review because it was never given to me.

The manager spoke to HR and came back a few days later. She shared with me that because HR and my previous manager did not deliver the final warning to me, it was null and void. She stated that if no further behaviors are demonstrated based on the past, I would be in the clear. I knew better. I had no intentions of going back and forth with any manager about the schedule again. The manager seemed to care about my performance and progress in the beginning, but shortly after, I saw differently. On several occasions the manager told me I should be in her role since I possess the knowledge to do so. It almost felt like she wanted me to do her job, and on many days, I did. The team often reached out to me if they had questions or concerns because when they asked our manager, she did not provide sufficient information. I was mentally and physically drained.

By December 2023, I was asking God to please let me make it to March since that was when we got our annual bonuses each year. I knew if I made it to March, I would resign from my role. It was beyond time. I was tired of doing my work and my manager's work. She never gave me any recognition for my efforts, and I was tired of being used. In addition to the team solely relying on me for help, I served as the team's liaison. When there was a concern among the team, I was the individual who communicated this information.

It essentially placed a target on my back. Working for a natural gas provider during the winter months was not for the weak. The call volume typically doubles during that time and customers have concerns about their high gas bills. In February 2024 during a very hectic high bill season, the Specialist Team started having several meetings with the Senior Leadership Team. During those meetings, I was the specialist doing most of the talking. After two meetings, I stopped talking as much and allowed others on the team to convey their concerns. The moment I stopped talking, the Senior Leadership Team wanted to know what was wrong. I simply told them I wanted to provide an opportunity for other teammates to express their concerns. I thought they understood. A few days later I was pulled into a meeting with my manager. She advised me to be mindful of how I come across in meetings. I was puzzled because I thought my delivery and communication was respectful and clear. She told me my communication could be perceived as loud, aggressive and unprofessional. Wow! Was that really the perception?

There were three senior leaders in the latest meetings. Therefore, I sent an email to each of them extending my sincere apologies for being loud, aggressive or unprofessional during our meetings. To my surprise, each of them called or stopped by my desk to tell me that was not the perception that they received from me at all. Surprised by their response, I was confused. My manager had warned me about being loud, aggressive and unprofessional but none of the senior leadership team had this perception of me.

This was such a red flag for me. Why did my manager tell me to be mindful of these things if it was not the true perception? Were these her thoughts and she was passing the blame to the Senior Leadership team? My manager's boss told me that my manager would pull me for a meeting soon. Days went by and she never spoke to me. The following day when we were in the office, she asked me to come to her desk for our one-on-one. With most of our one-on-one meetings we discuss performance. This meeting was different. She chastised me for sending an email that I did not copy her on. She felt like I went over her head instead of going to her first. I was baffled. I did not understand why she felt this way. She told me the Senior Leadership Team had a problem with my professionalism, tone and delivery. However, I later found out that it was not their perception at all. It seemed like it was hers. Instead of my manager owning up to her perception, she passed the blame to the Senior Leadership Team instead. I could not believe this.

My manager proved she was no longer trustworthy, and I moved accordingly. My eyes were wide open now. From that meeting until our last meeting on

April 23, 2024, things were different between us. She picked on me if she thought I did not speak to her. She picked on me if she thought I was not communicating with her enough. She questioned the reason behind everything I did or said. If I sat in a different area from the team instead of asking me, she asked the IT team. She was being messy. In March 2024, several employees were terminated due to unethical behavior. Two of the seven employees that were terminated were from the specialist team. Our team of seven was down to five team members.

Our leadership team had no interest in filling the two roles we lost. It was frustrating and concerning. We had recently fully staffed our team, and in a short time we were shorthanded again. April was a busy month of travel for me. Prior to losing teammates, I scheduled time off to attend my sister's wedding in Hawaii. In addition, I had two emergency dental appointments due to a broken bridge. I did not consider the team was short staffed because the paid time off (PTO) requests were submitted months in advance. On April 23, 2024, my manager called me into a meeting. Instead of asking if I could adjust my PTO requests or determining if there was a compromise, she accused me of taking PTO to avoid my closing shift. Working 10 a.m. – 7 p.m. was not an ideal shift for me because it impacted the things I did outside of GS. It meant I could not tutor my students, which impacted my finances. I was very defensive about the accusations because it was not what I was doing. My closing days were Mondays, Thursdays and Fridays. Supposedly, the individuals who created the schedules for us alerted the manager that all my requests were on days when I was scheduled to close.

The accusations were not true. I could not believe she was accusing me of something so trivial. I shared with her that I did not understand what was going on and why I was being targeted. Unfortunately, the entire specialist team became a target, but we did nothing wrong. She said okay, and we ended the meeting. Shortly after, she sent me a message in Microsoft Teams stating, "This is the same behavior that was addressed with you from your previous manager, correct?" I responded, "No, that was not accurate." I felt uneasy. Was she really trying to correlate what was going on now with the situation from my previous manager? It was unbelievable.

The next day when we were required to work in the office, the manager never talked to me. She conducted one-on-one meetings with all the other teammates except me. I remembered receiving an alert that my alarm was going off at home. After disarming the alarm, I discovered my front door was wide open. After sending a message via Microsoft Teams to let her know what happened, she sent me a message back asking if my home would be okay until I got off work. Was she serious? It was only noon, and I did not finish work until 5:00 p.m. Did she really expect me to leave the front door to my home open that long? I was livid.

Before I knew it, I broke down. I was so upset and angry. The tears would not stop flowing from my eyes. I reached out to my previous manager to talk. I shared with her what was going on. She asked me in the most polite tone, "Why are you still here at GS? You are so much bigger than this." She was right. March came and went. Bonuses were disappointing. Yet, I was still at GS when the plan was to resign in March. After receiving my annual bonus and not receiving the amount I expected, I decided to stay for a few more months until my 401K balance was over a certain amount. I knew the chances of me returning to a full-time job immediately after leaving GS were very slim. I knew I needed income to handle my monthly obligations. Therefore, I planned to cash out my 401K and pay up on some of my bills. I had a feasible plan, but God was tired of my disobedience.

I was disturbed by the way my manager treated me in the office, but it all made sense. On Thursday, April 25, 2024, my normal work from home day, I clocked in at 10 a.m. By 11:30 a.m., I was already scheduled for my first break. During my break I packed up headsets, keyboards, the second monitor, manuals, and anything that belonged to GS. I placed it in a box and moved it to the living room. I planned to work in office on Friday, April 26, 2024, so that I could release my equipment and resign. I was tired. As soon as I logged back in from break, I received a message via Microsoft Teams from the legal assistant who was formally the HR director. She wanted to know if I was available for a call.

When we joined the call, she shared with me how these calls are never easy, but she had to let me know I was being placed on paid administrative leave until an investigation was completed. My supervisor accused me of not participating in one meeting, using PTO to avoid my closing shift, and I had complaints internally from my peers. . Though we talked for over an hour regarding this matter, I simply asked her to do her due diligence and obtain the facts. I knew in my heart, I would not be returning as an employee when the investigation was completed. She told me I should expect a call back within five days, but no later than Tuesday, April 30, 2024. My administrative leave was effective immediately and my access to all programs were suspended. That meant the laptop I consistently used for everything was blocked. In that moment, I knew I needed a new laptop for personal use. When I hung up the phone, I shared with my son what was going on. He was upset and mentioned that it was not fair. I had to be strong despite how I felt so I kept my emotions to myself.

I was boiling inside. Surprisingly, instead of having a transparent conversation with me, my manager reported me to HR. That was crazy to me. The accusations were false. I did nothing wrong. However, in that moment I heard God say, "When I say move, that is what I mean." I received the same message when I was released from Ross. I was supposed to quit after my anxiety attack, but I did not. The Bible tells us in I Samuel 15:22, "And Samuel said, Hath the LORD as great delight in burnt offerings and sacrifices, as in obeying the voice of the LORD? Behold, to obey is better than sacrifice, and to hearken than the fat of rams." This Scripture tells us that God values obedience over ritual sacrifices. I knew in that moment, obedience was better than sacrifice, but I was taking my time doing what He told me to do.

Six days later, the legal assistant called me back to let me know I was released from my position at GS. In that moment I was numb, but relieved. I was finally free. She informed me that the company was prepared to offer me a severance package for the years spent working for the company. She encouraged me to consult with an attorney before deciding. She was very informative. She asked if I had any questions. The only question I asked was, "When could I drop off the equipment?" She told me she was not sure if boxes were still sent out to pack up equipment. I shared with her that I did not need a box because everything was already packed in a box. It took her by surprise, but none of that mattered to me.

I was wrongly released from my role, and although I did not want the position back, I was ready to fight. After speaking with a few attorneys and being reminded that Georgia is an at-will state, I decided to accept the severance package. An at-will state means employers do not need a reason to release an employee from their role. It is truly unfortunate, but these are things we deal with living in Georgia. Even though the way I was treated was wrong, I was grateful for the conclusion of this chapter. I thought the end of my journey with GS would come peacefully, but it did not. I received lots of calls and texts when former employees realized I was no longer with the company. There were many who felt I was treated unfairly, but there was nothing anyone could do. There were some individuals who called just to get information. A few individuals reached out to share their insight. While others genuinely wanted to know how I was doing.

As I attempted to move past this phase in my life, I knew I needed a fresh start and a reset. I needed to spend time away and talk to God. It was necessary to seek God for direction regarding my next steps. I needed Him to order my steps and to lead and guide me. The next move I made, I wanted God's total approval. A few days later I started planning my spiritual reset trip.

Initially, I did not know where I was going, but soon after, Dubai became my preferred destination. When I decided to travel to Dubai, the only person I told was my son. He asked several questions out of concern, but I reassured him God would be with me no matter where I went. In 2019, when I first planned to go to Dubai, none of my family members were okay with me traveling alone. It was a constant battle trying to convince them I would be okay. I was single during that time, but my relationship status never stopped me from traveling in the past. Unfortunately, I did not make it to Dubai in 2019. To avoid being discouraged about taking the trip this time, I did not tell my parents or friends I was going until the week before. Everyone understood and respected my decision. In the end, I had to take this trip for me.

After I booked my flight and accommodations, I did additional research to prepare for my trip. It was necessary for me to do my own research instead of relying solely on what I heard from others. There was a lot of information floating around about what women could or could not do. The clothing women were expected to wear was something I wanted to be prepared for. Since most of the clothes in my closet consist of skirts and dresses, I did not have to purchase much. I did order a matching abaya and hijab. These are items women wear when they go to the mosque. Since one of the stops on my list was to visit the Sheikh Zayed Grand Mosque, it was essential to purchase these items. It is such a sacred place – the largest mosque in the United Arab Emirates - and I wanted to experience it. Therefore, I planned accordingly to ensure I respect their rules and culture.

This would provide me with an opportunity to talk to and hear from God. It was the perfect time to sit still and listen. I was in a space where I needed to hear from Him. I needed Him to lead and guide me. I needed God to order my steps for what was to come in my life. In addition to spending uninterrupted time with God, my trip to Dubai would be a great opportunity to start writing my third book. I was excited to embark on this journey. I booked all the experiences for Dubai during the planning phase. I scheduled two tours and a flying dress photo shoot. The tours included a full day in Abu Dhabi with lunch and a half day tour in Dubai with a visit to the tallest building, Burj Khalifa. These were all once-in-a-lifetime experiences that I was grateful for.

On Sunday, May 26, 2024, after attending church with my family and them giving me their love, I left for my spiritual reset trip to Dubai. Before boarding my flight, I talked to God. While awaiting departure, I had a conversation with God again. I was at peace knowing He would watch over and protect me. I was in a good space mentally, and for that I was grateful. I was ready to open my eyes and clearly observe the things God placed in front of me.

On the way to Dubai, our first stop was Paris, France. I expected a 90-minute layover. However, when we arrived it was time to go straight to our gate. I did not realize that even though I never went outside the airport,

I would have to go through the security checkpoint again. By the time I got through the checkpoint in France, I was running to my gate to ensure I did not miss my flight. Thank God I was working out regularly with my trainer so the sprint to my gate did not leave me out of breath. I was appreciative of that small miracle. I made it to my gate before the plane departed. After I boarded my flight, we experienced a two-hour delay. There was a problem with luggage, which resulted in a major delay. I patiently waited and realized God was in complete control.

When I arrived in Dubai, it was very late. I checked my bag, so I had to wait for my luggage to arrive at baggage claim. I was so happy to see my luggage come down the conveyor belt. I experience a bit of anxiety when it comes to checking my bags, because my bag was left in another state previously. However, seeing my luggage eased the anxiety. I was relieved. It was close to midnight when I finally scheduled an Uber from the airport. Dubai was eight hours ahead of Atlanta, so I was already off schedule. My photo shoot was scheduled at 7 a.m., which meant I had to be dressed and ready to meet my driver by 6:15 a.m. As soon as I checked into my hotel, I took a shower and went to sleep. I was exhausted. Thankfully, I got some rest and was ready for my photo shoot. The longest part of the phot shoot was the drive. The flying dress shoot on the desert was quite an experience. The dress was beautiful which the photographer provided. She also helped me get dressed and prepared for the shoot. Within 20-30 minutes, the shoot was completed, and we headed back to my hotel.

We returned to the hotel sooner than expected so I had time for a quick nap. My next adventure started at 10 a.m. and I would get a chance to visit the Grand Mosque. I was truly grateful for the opportunity. I said my prayers and went to sleep. An hour later my alarm went off letting me know it was time to get up and get dressed. I got dressed and hurried to the lobby to meet my driver. He introduced himself and told me where we were going. This would be a full day tour starting at 10 a.m. and ending around 8 p.m. I was excited. Our first stop was the Grand Mosque, and it was better than I expected.

The security team made sure everyone followed the rules regarding their attire. No one was mean or harsh. The Grand Mosque was very beautiful. There were several opportunities for pictures and lots of people were there. One thing I would have liked to experience was an actual prayer at the mosque. Though there were several moments of silence during the tour, having an encounter with God in such a sacred place would have been such a wonderful experience. Thankfully, I am not restricted to locations when it comes to encounters with God. I can be at home, church, in my car, out of town, anywhere. He is always with me. Once we left the Grand Mosque, it was lunch time. My tour guide took me to a preferred restaurant so I could eat. After lunch, we stopped at a few more places before I started feeling bad. I was not sure if I was just tired and needed to rest or if it was something I ate. After a few more stops, I asked the tour guide to take me back to my hotel.

When I got back to my hotel, I said my prayers and went to sleep. When I woke up, I felt a lot better. I was obviously tired and just needed rest. I wanted to walk to the Dubai Mall since it was in walking distance to my hotel. However, I wanted to take it easy since I had been moving nonstop since I arrived in Dubai. Instead of going to the mall, I relaxed by the pool. It was such a relaxing and refreshing experience. The buildings and views in Dubai were breathtaking. The Dubai Fountain was amazing. It was an attraction at the Dubai Mall, but from my hotel I could experience the lights, music, and water show every 30 minutes starting at 6 p.m. I loved it. It provided me an opportunity to observe and witness the goodness of God. I was truly in awe. I was filled with so much gratitude. I was in disbelief. I finally made it to a place that was at the top of my list to visit since 2019. God is so good. He is faithful through it all. After spending several hours at the pool and being at peace, I walked back to my room, and prepared for bed. I packed my luggage, took a shower, and climbed in bed. The next morning, I had my final tour with a new tour guide. When I checked out of my hotel, they offered to hold my luggage while I went on my final tour. I was grateful I did not have to keep up with my luggage all day. When my tour guide arrived, he greeted me in the lobby. He asked me if I wanted to bring my luggage, and I told him since my flight was later in the evening it was best to leave it at the hotel.

Our first stop was The Burji Khalifa, which is known for being the tallest building in world since 2009. The Burji Khalifa stands at 2,722 ft. tall. I was nervous initially because I have a fear of heights. In addition, I have a history of motion sickness. I quickly learned we would take an elevator to the top of the building. I did not know how fast the elevator would go or if I would be able to see outside while we traveled to the top. I refused to let fear settle in. I said a quick prayer and knew God was with me.

When I joined the line, there were several people waiting for their opportunity to get to the top. When the elevator came down, it was our time to go up. Surprisingly, when we got in the elevator, it was dark. Once we started moving, which did not seem to be going fast, the elevator provided a light show of how the building was formed. It was a very interesting way to capture our attention and take our mind off just how fast and high we were going. When we got to the top, we walked out of the elevator to all the beautiful sights of Dubai. It was truly amazing. I did not experience any motion sickness, and the fear of being so high was no longer an issue. It was a great photo opportunity. We went up 124 levels by elevator and walked up to level 125. I enjoyed capturing the memories, getting professional pictures made, and purchasing souvenirs to take back home. The best part about the experience was I did not experience any motion sickness. God was taking care of me through it all.

When my tour was over at The Burj Khalifa, I stopped for lunch. Instead of rushing back to the car and eating on the way, my tour guide allowed me to eat my food in the food court at the mall. It provided an opportunity for me to see some of the stores in the Dubai

Mall. Once I finished eating, we walked back to the car. We were scheduled to go to "Old Dubai" and learn about its history. Unfortunately, the car did not start which resulted in a more than two- hour delay leaving the mall. It was okay because things often happen beyond our control. My only problem was my iPhone's battery was low, and I had no way to charge my phone until we got back in the car. My tour guide did not want me to wait with him in the heat, so he suggested I go back to the mall lobby. Since I had my laptop and the mall had free Wi-Fi, I was able to get some writing done while I waited. In addition, I remembered my new laptop bag had a USB port which allowed me to charge my phone. LOOK AT GOD! He shows out every single time. Even though my tour was delayed, it provided me an opportunity to get some writing done and charge my phone at the same time.

After some time passed, my tour guide came back to get me, and we left. We stopped at a few places along the way which included the Dubai Marina, Jumeriah Burj Al Arab, and Dubai Gold Souk. I enjoyed every minute. My tour guide was very personable and informative. He wanted to make sure I saw all the places we were scheduled to see before his car would not start. We stopped by the parts store to purchase a new battery. Once he got the new battery, we had no more issues with the car. Regardless of the minor delay, I had a great time.

When I got back to my hotel to retrieve my luggage, I sat in the lobby for a little while before heading to the airport. I could not believe my trip to Dubai was coming to an end. I had such an unforgettable experience, and I was overwhelmed with pure joy. I took an Uber back to the airport. I checked my luggage and prayed that it would arrive with me in Atlanta. When I attempted to get through the security checkpoint, I was told I had to stop by customs. A little nervous, I followed instructions and did what I was told. When I got to customs, they needed to stamp my passport. When you travel to Dubai, you receive an arrival stamp upon entry and an exit stamp upon departure. I had no further challenges getting to my gate. While I sat at my gate waiting to leave Dubai, I said another prayer and thanked God for keeping me safe and protected. Dubai was one of the safest places I had the pleasure of visiting. Yes, it is a male dominant country, but the men give the upmost respect to women. It was safe. No one locked their car doors. Dubai had little to no crime. It was such a rewarding experience, and if it is God's will, I will go back.

After about six hours in flight, we stopped in Amsterdam for our final layover before heading back to Atlanta. Like when we stopped in France, there was not much of a wait before it was time to board out flight. I was happy to finally see another Delta flight crew and plane. The flight back to Atlanta was so peaceful. The flight was half full of a very big plane so many travelers were on a row by themselves. I was on a row by myself, and I was so happy. It provided me with an opportunity to rest without being disturbed. The flight crew barely served food, drinks or snacks on our flight because everyone was sleeping and declined service. When we arrived safely in Atlanta, I was overwhelmed with gratitude. God had taken me from Atlanta to Dubai and brought me home safely with no hurt, harm or danger. I was overjoyed.

My family was also grateful for traveling grace and mercy. Traveling to Dubai was my furthest trip to date. In addition, it was the furthest trip that I traveled alone. If I had to do it all over again, I would do it alone. The trip to Dubai allowed me to observe things God wanted me to see without distractions. He wanted to show me that He was in complete control because He has all power in His hands. It was also a reminder that I do not have to fear because He is always with me.

CHAPTER 2 LESSON

There are times when God must separate us from others to get our attention. It is so easy to get caught up in things and take our eyes off God. It is important that we are intentional about hearing what He is saying to us and clearly observing those things He needs us to see. Take some time to talk to God and truly be obedient when He shows you things. It will change your life. I know from experience that it is not always easy to do or go immediately where God is leading you. However, God will never do anything to hurt us and that is only confirmation we need to know that God is always with us. We must learn to observe clearly what he is showing us.

OBEDIENCE

Chapter 3

OBEDIENCE TEST

Obedience is defined as compliance with a request, order or law. This simply means obeying an order, law, or request the first time it is given. Obedience is also defined as submission to another's authority. From a spiritual perspective, obedience means to hear, trust, submit and surrender to God and His word. This is essential on my spiritual walk with God, but I still struggle with this. The Bible tells us in James 1:22 (KJV), "But be ye doers of the word, and not hearers only, deceiving your own selves." This Scripture tells us to act on the word that we hear from God without fear. Recent circumstances have allowed me to acknowledge my shortcomings when it comes to being obedient to God.

In February 2024, work at GS was extremely stressful. I had enough. I was mentally drained. I felt undervalued and unappreciated. The calls were nonstop. The customers were difficult to please. Not to mention we were under so much pressure due to all the changes within the company. It was a lot to deal with. When I logged off work each day unless I had to tutor my students, I went straight to sleep. I said to God one day, "Please let me make it to March so I could get my annual bonus and then leave." When March arrived and we received our annual bonus, I was extremely disappointed. After receiving over $10,000 two years in a row, bonuses decreased significantly, even though the company made more money. It was very disappointing.

I did not know what I was going to do. As soon as I received my bonus and paid a few things off, those funds were gone. I could not possibly leave GS, especially without having a new job. It was the first time I heard the Holy Spirit tell me to leave. Despite what I heard, I remained at GS and came up with a plan that I thought would work. I decided to cash out my 401K and use those funds to pay things off. When I checked my balance in my 401K account, I determined it was not enough. I decided I would stay at GS for two more months before submitting my resignation. Again, the Holy Spirit told me to leave.

I thought if I stayed for just a little while longer, I would obtain the finances I needed to survive while I looked for a new job. God was not pleased with my disobedience. Often, God will give us grace until He says, "Enough is enough." Luke 12:47 (KJV) tells us, "And that servant who knew his Lord's will, and prepared not himself, neither did according to his will, shall be beaten

with many stripes." I was disobedient. I knew my
punishment would come soon if I did not obey His word.

God told me twice to leave GS, and I did not. I
allowed fear to keep me in another role that was stressful,
and it impacted my mental health. In addition to worrying
about my finances, I was worried about losing health and
dental insurance for my son and me. Since I started
working 25 years ago, I consistently maintained health,
dental, and life insurance for us. It was a necessity. I never
wanted to be in a position to need it and not have it, so I
maintained those coverages by any means necessary. I
was concerned that if I did not have a full-time job, I
would not have the coverage we needed.

There was so much going through my mind
during that time. Not only would I be without adequate
income, but I would lose our insurance coverage as well.
What was I going to do? I needed income. I needed health,
dental, and life insurance. Maintaining a full-time job
over the years has allowed me to maintain those
coverages. Honestly, I did not know another way. Due to
my lack of research, fear caused me to be disobedient and
doubt the power of God. I knew He was tired of waiting
for me to do what He asked me to do. Therefore, though
being placed on administrative leave did not surprise me,

being wrongly released did. God reminded me again, "When I say move, that is what I expect you to do." I hung my head down because I knew I was disobedient. As a result of my disobedience, I was going through the challenge of being wrongly released from a company that I dedicated my life to for 10 years.

Though I no longer wanted to remain in that role, I was concerned about adequate insurance and income. God was already working things out for me, even in my disobedience. I have never worked at a job where a company paid severance to an employee who did something wrong. If I did something wrong which resulted in releasing me from my role, financial compensation would not be necessary. However, in my case I was offered a severance package. GS offered a week of pay for the number of years I was employed plus the employer paid portion of my insurance if I decided to enroll in COBRA, also known as continuation of health coverage.

I was grateful to God for what He was already doing in my life. In addition, my plan was to cash out my 401K and use those resources to pay bills for a few months. That was the plan before I was released from my role. Again, I allowed fear to keep me from stepping out on faith and trusting God. Even though I lost $10,000 for cashing out my 401K, I got it right back when my severance was paid out from GS. I was able to pay bills off and in advance as I planned. I was in awe of what God was doing for me. Before May 2024 was over, I accomplished so much. I purchased a cash car for my son, paid off credit cards, paid rent and other household bills for a few months. In addition, I was able to secure health, dental, and life insurance for my son and me before the month ended. I was grateful to God because He was with me every step of the way.

Even in my disobedience, God was still working things out for me. I was at peace. I was no longer overwhelmed or stressed out. I was no longer logging off work each day and going to sleep because I was emotionally drained. For the first time in a while, I was not worried about my finances. I was not worried about finding a new job. I was focused on building my tutoring business -Dr. Marci Nspirations Group LLC - and growing my non-profit organization. I was still pretty busy, but grateful I was no longer clocking in on someone else's clock. I was blessed.

My obedience was tested again in 2022 when God placed it on my heart to launch a non-profit organization. After dealing with very minimal support over the years, I wanted to create a space where women felt supported, safe and celebrated. In addition, I wanted us to serve and give back to our communities. After bouncing the idea around with one of my Sista friends, she felt it was a good idea. She shared that it was a resource many women needed. I thought about it briefly and never acted on my thoughts. In August 2023, the idea came to me again. I spoke to another Sista friend and asked her thoughts. She was very excited and supportive of the idea. Even with the initial support, I was still hesitant to do what God asked me to do.

In November 2023, while I was scrolling on my business Instagram page, I ran across a celebrity's page who recently launched her latest business venture. "Wow! Look at this!" I thought to myself. The entire concept was the same passion I had for my organization. From the name of the organization to the events and purpose, it fully matched my vision. In that moment, I acknowledged God and said, "I hear you." I immediately went to my Google calendar and set an alert to brainstorm S.I.S. (Selebrating in Sisterhood LLC) the next day at 7 a.m. Ironically, I already knew the name of the organization two years prior. Besides the name and the purpose, I had no other details regarding the organization.

On November 25, 2023, I woke up and went to work brainstorming. Within a few short hours, I had a tentative vision, purpose and tagline. I knew what colors I wanted for the logo and the visual concept. I determined what resources the organization would offer. I wanted the organization to provide a mentorship program for girls ages 12-18. This is such a critical age for girls and young women. Therefore, ensuring they have the support they need is essential. Since the organization would be a new business, I knew the funding I needed to run the business would be very minimal. That is when I decided to implement membership fees. Affordability was my top priority. I wanted to implement fees that members felt were affordable and worth the investment each month. I developed two tier levels: tier one and top tier. Tier one provides monthly communication, access to one event monthly, and access to organizational resources. I set the cost for this tier at $15 a month. Top tier provides monthly communication, access to all organizational sponsored events, access to organizational resources, a t-shirt, and other branded items. This tier is $20 a month. After I prayed and talked to God about the decisions I made, I started on the paperwork. I knew I wanted the organization to be listed as a legit business in the state of Georgia.

I went to the Georgia Secretary of State website and applied for the business formation. This process lets an individual know if they can use the name they selected for the business. It is usually a very seamless and quick process. I have formed a few businesses in the State of Georgia, so I am almost an expert. As of December 1, 2023, the SIS Organization was officially recognized as a business in Georgia. Once I received approval, I went to the IRS website and applied for an employer identification number (EIN). The EIN was essential to open a business checking account. I was intentional about setting up the organization correctly.

I explored a few banks to determine what would be the best option with minimal fees. I decided on PNC Bank for the business checking account. The branch manager was very helpful and insightful. He made the process seamless. I was grateful. Things were falling into place effortlessly, and I was overwhelmed with joy. God was working things out for me as I knew He would.

I contacted a graphic designer on Fiverr to develop a logo. Within just a few short days, I had a logo

I was proud of. After I received the final files for the logo, I created a website, set up a business address, obtained a business phone number, and created a Google profile. After the major components were complete, I scheduled information sessions via Zoom. The sessions provided an opportunity for individuals to learn about the organization, vision, purpose, membership fees, mentorship program, and upcoming launch event. I held two successful information sessions before I got sick and had to cancel the last one. I could not recall the last time I was sick with a cold. However, I knew it had been a while. When I got sick, it felt like the enemy wanted to slow me down. I was finally being obedient to what God told me to do and the enemy did not like that. Even though I had to put planning on pause for a few weeks, I came back stronger than ever.

The number of women who were interested in the organization amazed me. I was grateful. I quickly learned that not only were the women interested, but they were committed as well. Many believed in the vision and purpose of the organization. The vision I developed was: "To create a powerful network of women positively influencing the world through selebration, service, support and sisterhood." The mission I created for the organization is: "To authentically equip, empower, and encourage women through service, support, selebration and sisterhood." It was important for me to create a safe space with positive, passionate, like-minded and authentic women.

There were so many women who did not have that. They did not have a strong circle of women they could depend on when things were good, bad, happy, sad, frustrating or rewarding. Each woman I talked to needed that type of support, and I wanted to provide it through the SIS organization. It was important for me to establish that kind of sisterhood because I needed it. In December 2014 after I graduated with my bachelor's degree in English, I felt it was time to celebrate. My parents were very proud and felt that celebrating was a great idea. Not only did I want to celebrate with my family, I wanted to celebrate with all the individuals who I thought genuinely supported me. I learned quickly that those who I supported did not support me authentically. I spent a lot of money to cover the cost of the venue, invitations, party favors, balloons, food, and supplies. I invited almost 100 people, but only about 20 people showed up for me. I was heartbroken and devastated.

The day of the event was very hard for me. It seemed like every hour I received a call that someone could not make it, or a text message telling me something came up. This was one of many moments where I realized the support I gave was not reciprocated. I was so disappointed that I cried. I did not understand why people did not show up for me the way I showed up for them. It was the lack of support over the years that fueled my passion to create the SIS organization. I wanted women to feel supported in every aspect of their lives. I wanted to selebrate women authentically. In addition, I wanted to create a powerful network of women who were committed to service. Being able to give back to the communities we live in was vital. The women were genuinely excited about the organization because of the value it would bring to their lives.

I created a membership form for acceptance into the SIS organization. This allowed me to vet and find the right women to be a part of the powerful network I was building. The membership form was very brief but asked thought-provoking questions. Anyone seeking acceptance into the SIS organization had to complete it. No exceptions. Reviewing the completed forms helped me to determine if that person was a good fit for the organization. I was looking for key words in each response. This was critical when deciding who should be accepted. Once a member was accepted into the organization, membership fees were due. There were no concerns or complaints about the monthly membership fees. Things fell into place very well.

I decided I wanted to do an official launch for the SIS organization late January 2024. I did not know what that would look like due to limited funds. By the first week of January, there were nine women who were accepted into the SIS organization. They were very excited and committed to embark on this journey with me. Initially, we started with 10 women, but one decided she could not commit to the organization due to other obligations. Even though I understood, for a brief moment I was discouraged. I thought the vision that God birthed inside me would fail. Fear slowly crept in. I knew I could not let God down by being disobedient, so I moved forward knowing He was with me. I was also reminded by an associate that I had nine women who were already signed up and committed. She reassured me that was something to be proud of and I was. I was so grateful.

Since I knew the number of women attending the launch would be nine, it allowed me to adequately plan.

Once I determined where the launch would be held, I decided on food, drinks, decorations, and gifts for members. I ordered personalized sugar cookies and chocolate covered strawberries to match the theme and colors. Things were falling into place so well. I was very happy. One of the best parts about planning the SIS launch is that I used all mall Black-owned businesses to help me execute the launch. It was important for me to keep the business in our communities.

Since things were going so well, I decided to do something special for the members. The logo that was created for the website was also used for the very first SIS shirt. None of the members anticipated shirts because the organization was newly formed. However, I wanted to add something else to the gift bags. These nine women meant everything to me. Not only were they the first to commit to the organization, but they also supported me in everything overall. These women were authentic and transparent. It was truly a blessing to have them in my life and now a part of the SIS organization.

After I ordered the shirts for the SIS launch, I dropped them off to have the logo added. Freddyo's Tees & Quote is a black-owned business in the heart of Atlanta that never disappoints. I have utilized their services for years. I am always satisfied. When I decided to execute this project with the business, I knew the final product would meet my expectations. Within a few days, the shirts were complete, and I was proud. The SIS Organization officially had a shirt, and I was very excited. As things continued to fall into place for the SIS launch, I knew God was leading and guiding me.

On Sunday, January 28, 2024, I held the official SIS Launch. It was a huge success, and everything was beautiful. The location, décor, food, energy, party favors, and connections made were phenomenal. The icebreaker activities allowed members to get to know one another a little better and were hilarious. After introductions, we started working on our vision boards. I decided at the last minute to include vision boards because most of the members had never completed one or had not created one for 2024. It was a great opportunity to manifest realistic goals for the year. I created an agenda for the launch so we could stay on schedule. At the end of the event, all members assisted with clean up and breakdown. There was not much I had to do upon their departure, but rest. In addition, I requested that all members take the remaining food home so I would not have to. They did just that.

The next day, I started planning for what was next for the organization. I knew monthly meetings would be an essential part of the SIS Organization to keep members informed. Meetings would provide an opportunity to communicate important updates about the organization, briefly recap any events, discuss upcoming events, and obtain suggestions and feedback from members. Things were going smoothly. Shortly after the launch, I realized I needed additional support. I believed the SIS organization would continue to grow, and I wanted things to be ran well and organized. I decided I needed a leadership team. This team would assist and support me in managing the SIS organization.

In just a short time, I created four additional roles for the SIS organization which included chief operating officer, SIS lead coordinator, SIS events coordinator, and SIS mentorship program coordinator. Members who were interested in serving in a role had to complete an interest form and share what skills they would bring to that role. Initially, the interest in leadership roles was very limited. Not many members expressed interest. After I provided more explanation for each role, the interest increased. Ironically, there were more members interested in being the mentorship coordinator than any other role. As a result, I added an additional leadership role which included the SIS assistant. This role completed the SIS leadership team. After each individual was appointed to a leadership role, everyone was reintroduced to the organization. It meant so much that I had a team willing to work beside me and run the SIS organization. I knew this was just the beginning.

In addition to monthly meetings with the SIS members, the leadership team implemented monthly meetings as well. These meetings would be held to collaborate on new ideas, suggestions, fundraising efforts, recommendations, and donor and sponsor options. It would also provide leaders an opportunity to connect on important topics before sharing with the rest of the organization. All meetings were held virtually because it is the most convenient option. By June 2024, the SIS organization held six successful events with the rest of the year planned. Membership grew from nine members to 18. Two members were considered our Little SIS (LSIS) because they are participating in our LSIS S2S Mentorship Program. Despite a strong start to the SIS organization, there were a few members who had to be removed because they were no longer the right fit. After much prayer and wanting to be obedient to God's word, these individuals were removed. I was not discouraged because I knew God giveth and he taketh away.

Since the birth of the SIS organization came directly from God, it was vital that I remained obedient to his word. During the initially planning stages, I considered an individual for the organization who I knew God was not pleased with. He told me clearly "No." After extending an invitation to an info session and being ignored, it further confirmed why God told me "No." I never asked or suggested again. I was building a powerful, positive, authentic network of women who believed in pouring into each other, praising one another, and praying for each other genuinely. I could not let individuals join who would impact this vision. I had to remain selective when it came to accepting new members into the organization to ensure there were no issues.

One of the most memorable moments with the organization so far was our SIS Volunteer Day. Several members & leaders volunteered at the Atlanta Community Food Bank in East Point, Georgia. We arrived promptly for our session, gave our canned good donations, completed registration, and attended volunteer orientation. Shortly after orientation, we were assigned to different stations within the warehouse where we sorted food for three hours. It was very inspiring working as a team to sort through food to ensure those less fortunate would have something to eat. It was very humbling and fun. Besides some heat concerns, everything went well.

In March 2024, the organization held the first SIS Pamper Day. This event provided members with an opportunity to relax and unwind for the afternoon with music, food, drinks and massages. It was perfect. Each member received a personalized robe with the SIS logo. Everyone enjoyed themselves and found value in creating time to simply relax. In July 2024, the organization held the first SIS Family and Fun Day. This event provided an opportunity for members to bring their significant others and kids for a day of food, fun and family. To take the load off one person, each member agreed to bring something to contribute to the event. We had plenty of food, drinks, snacks, chips, desserts, fruit and a cake. Besides a few concerns with flies and other critters, the event was a huge success.

As the SIS organization continues to grow, I have no doubt that God will continue to lead and guide me on this journey. I refuse to let anyone, or anything come in the way of what God has birthed inside me. I am grateful to have a powerful network of women pouring into each other, praising one another, and praying genuinely for each individual daily. This is a result of being obedient to God.

CHAPTER 3 LESSON

As we know, obedience is better than sacrifice, which means we should choose to be obedient in every situation we encounter. Fear causes us to be disobedient, but God will never leave us nor forsake us. Therefore, we already have the power inside us to do anything we need to do with His help. Besides, if God be for us, who can be against us. It will be critical on this spiritual journey to step out on faith and know God is with us.

OBEDIENCE

Chapter 4

OBSTACLES TEST

Throughout life we will all encounter trials, tribulations and obstacles. Trials are considered things or situations that test a person's endurance. Tribulations refer to experiences that are hard to bear. Obstacles represent things or individuals who block one's way, prevents, or hinders progress. Many times, these things happen beyond our control. Other times, these things happen because of ongoing issues or challenges at home, with our kids, significant other, parents, etc.

I strongly believe trials, tribulations and obstacles come to make us stronger and strengthen our relationship with God. The Bible tells us in John 16:33 (KJV), "These things I have spoken unto you, that in me ye might have peace. In the world ye shall have tribulation: but be of good cheer; I have overcome the world." God tells us that even though we will experience trials, tribulations, and obstacles, we will overcome because He is with us. When we are amid the storm, it is hard to see just how we will overcome, but we will with the help of the LORD. During my life from childhood to adulthood, I have endured trials, tribulations and obstacles. Many were beyond my control, while others were a result of challenges happening in my home. Regardless to those instances, how I handled them made the difference.

In late June 2024, my significant other, DE, and I were scheduled to fly to Vegas to spend time with his dad. It would be my first time meeting him in person, so I was looking forward to the trip. The plan was for DE and me to meet at the airport since we did not live in the same home. His vehicle was a high target for break-ins at the airport, so the plan was to leave his vehicle at home. Since we had not discussed any changes, I assumed that was still the plan. After parking at Peachy Airport Parking and taking the shuttle to the airport, I arrived safely to South Terminal at Hartsfield Jackson International Airport. To my surprise, the airport was very busy for a Saturday morning. Delta curbside check-in was busy with a very long line. When I discovered how busy the airport was, I called DE immediately to determine where he was. His sense of urgency was never good when it came to traveling, so I was worried. He did not answer. I called right back. There was still no answer. I looked at the time and realized he still had over an hour to arrive.

I could not worry about him in that moment because I needed to check my bag and get through checkpoint. As I waited impatiently to get through curbside check in, it was finally my turn to check my bag. Once my bag was checked in, I texted DE to determine where he was. As I moved through a very busy checkpoint with long lines, again I wondered where he was. There was still no response from my text. I tried to ignore the knot that was forming in the pit of my stomach, but it would not go away. I was officially worried about DE. I made it all the way to the gate and still had not heard from him. He still had time to make it, so I tried to relax.

As soon as the gate agent announced pre-boarding and DE had not made it to the gate, I was very concerned. I did not know where he was or what was going on. There were several failed attempts to reach him by phone and texts. Despite not being able to reach him, I tried to remain calm. Once my zone was called to board the flight, the knot in my stomach got worse. Where was he? Once I got to my row, I took my seat and waited. A few minutes after boarding the plane, DE texted and asked me to send his boarding pass. After explaining to him that it was not something I could do, he called. He asked me to tell the flight attendants that he was one stop away from the terminal. I calmly asked, "what was the reason for the delay?" I did not understand why he enjoyed living on the edge when it came to traveling. He is always closer to missing flights than making them. I am the complete opposite. If I am supposed to be at the airport two or three hours before, I will be there at minimum of two or three hours before.

After waiting for his response and not getting it, I asked again, "why were you delayed getting here?" He responded, "Bessie is gone." My mind did not process the words fast enough, so I said, "Huh?" He calmly repeated again, "Bessie is gone." Shocked to hear this, I asked what happened. Bessie was his new 2023 Dodge Charger, scat pack, wide body, and fully loaded car he just purchased a year prior. He admitted that he was rushing to get to the airport and the roads were wet due to the rain. As a result of speed and wet roads, it caused him to lose control of the car and hit the median. "My God, are you okay?" I asked. "Let us forget about the car for a second, because it can be replaced." The most important thing for me was making sure he was okay. While I was talking to him on the phone, another passenger entered our row to claim his seat. I explained to her that the seat was taken, but the flight attendant told me the seat had been released. I was a bit bothered that Delta released a seat that was paid for, but I accepted the fact that DE was running behind schedule.

When he finally got to the gate, he was told he would not make the flight. Initially, I planned to get off the flight, but realized my bag was already on the plane. Therefore, I decided to remain on the flight. I told DE I loved him and would see him when he got to Vegas. I could not believe all of this was happening. I was grateful to God he was okay, but this was an obstacle we would have to tackle when we got back to Atlanta. After two flights and several hours later, DE made it safely to Vegas. I hugged him so tightly, because I was grateful he was ok after the car accident. He explained the thing that hurt the most was his feelings, and I completely understood.

Our time in Vegas came to an end quickly, and we were headed back to Atlanta together. We had such a great time with his dad and other family members. We were already planning a return trip before October if we could make it back.

On Wednesday morning, July 3, 2024, I was headed to the hair salon for a 9 a.m. appointment. It was the last opportunity I had to get my hair done before the SIS Family & Fun Day that upcoming Sunday, July 7th. I left home in sufficient time, so I was not rushing. I got off the exit at Washington Road in East Point, Georgia around 8:30 a.m. I was only five minutes away from the hair salon at that time. As I proceeded to go through the green light, there was a loud BOOM! I screamed so loud I scared myself. I had no idea what was going on. I looked around in total shock because I could not believe what had just happened. My airbags deployed. My car was sitting on the sidewalk. There was smoke everywhere. The car finally came to a stop after hitting a sign. What was going on? In that moment, I was in shock and disbelief. My mind had not yet processed that I was involved in a car accident.

The adrenaline I felt in that moment was vast. My head was pounding. My heart was racing. There was noticeable pain in my chest. Blood seemed to be everywhere. It was on my hand, my airbags, and my leg. I started looking around frantically to see what happened. I was confused. I immediately tried to get out the car. My driver's door would not open. Was it stuck? I was scared. The bracelets that I was wearing on my wrists popped. The beads were scattered all over the floor. I was still in shock so I begin to panic. The panic intensified when I attempted to get out the car a second time and was unable to do so. The fear took over me.

Was I going to die? Did someone see what happened? Was someone coming to help me? As I frantically attempted to get out my car, I started to cry. I was in so much pain climbing from the driver's seat to the passenger seat that I sat back down in the seat and started screaming, "Someone please help me! I am stuck in my car! Please help me!" Shortly after, I noticed a guy walking around the front of my car asking if I was okay. I immediately shouted, "I am stuck in my car! Please help me!" When I got to the passenger side, there was a tree preventing me from opening the door. I was in too much pain to climb to the back of my car, so I waited. Within a few short seconds, the guy was able to pry the door open so I could get out. I thanked him several times for helping me get out my car.

As soon as I got out the car, I realized my cellphones, wallet, ID, debit cards, credit cards, and all the things I needed were scattered all over the floor. I sat back down in the seat, grabbed what I could, and got out the car again. The guy who helped me get out the car asked me if I was okay. I told him, looking at my car with tears falling from my eyes, my car was gone. He said to me, "It is okay, YOU ARE ALIVE." In that moment, I finally realized I was involved in a car accident and God spared my life. Though I was still delusional and confused, it took me a moment to thank God for protecting me.

There was already a police officer onsite, but I did not realize how he arrived so quickly. When he came over to talk to me, I asked him where the third car was. He looked at me and said, "The car you hit is right there." I looked at him and said, "The car I hit was an SUV and it was rose gold." He said, "No, the car you hit was black and it is over there." I was so confused. All I remember seeing upon impact was a rose gold color and what appeared to be an SUV. He reassured me again that there were only two cars involved and the other driver pulled out in front of me. The officer admitted the other driver was at fault. I was just relieved someone knew what happened, because I was clueless. As I continued talking with the officer, I said to him, "Maybe it was the airbag I saw at impact." At that moment, I looked into my car and saw the color of my airbags were a rose color, which explains why I thought the car I hit was rose gold.

Even though I was beginning to piece together certain details of the accident, I still did not know what happened. I never saw the car before impact. It was such a scary moment for me. The officer mentioned that he called the police because it was outside of his jurisdiction.

By that time, I started noticing more blood, bruises, and the severe pain I was experiencing in my chest. It was difficult to stand without bending over because my chest was hurting so badly. I asked the officer if he could call an ambulance for me. He mentioned they were already on the way. After speaking to the officer, I looked at my car again. I knew it was totaled. It was bad. My entire engine was crushed like a soda can. My battery was laying in the middle of the street. I looked at the car and was overwhelmed with gratitude to be standing there.

I had to call my hair stylist to let her know I would not make it to the shop due to the accident. I immediately called DE to let him know I was involved in a car accident, four short days after he totaled his car. I could not reach him. I called my mother, but she did not answer. Instead, she texted and said she was busy at work. I texted her back and told her it was an emergency. I provided pictures of my car so she would understand the severity of my call.

I called my son, Alijah, so I could tell him what was going on. When he answered the phone, I could tell he was sleeping. Therefore, I tried to remain very calm while I explained what happened. I did not want him to panic. As soon as I mentioned that I was involved in a bad car accident, he was on high alert. He immediately asked if the location he had for me was accurate. Since we both have an iPhone, we share our locations with each other daily. I confirmed the accuracy of the location and provided specific instructions on how to get to me. I was extremely grateful. Alijah was the only one who answered my call the first time.

When my sone arrived, he helped me get all my personal things out of the car. He kept asking if I was okay while trying to remain calm. I told him I was in a lot of pain and needed to go to the hospital. He suggested I sit down in his car while he gathered everything from my car. While I waited for the East Point police officer to release my driver's license, the paramedics checked me out to ensure I was okay. After cleaning some of the cuts and scratches, I signed the release declining transport to the emergency room. I reassured them my son would drive me to the emergency room as soon as we left.

My mom called back very upset that I had been involved in a car accident. She left work immediately and told me she would meet us at the emergency room. The East Point police officer never spoke to me directly. He released my driver's license to Alijah and told him we were free to go. At that point, I was still confused about what happened. Why was I involved in a car accident? What could I have done to avoid it? Even though the first officer told me the other driver pulled out in front of me, I never saw the car before impact. I do know at some point I swerved because the car ended up on the sidewalk. Later, I determined the first officer on the scene was a Fulton County police officer. That is why he called an East Point officer because it was out of his jurisdiction. Despite being out of his jurisdiction, he remained on the scene with us until help arrived.

Alijah drove me straight to the emergency room. Thankfully, there was very minimum traffic on the highway, so we arrived quickly. I told Alijah I wanted to go to WellStar at Cobb since it was close to our home. Upon arrival, I shared with the triage nurse that I was in a lot of pain due to an automobile accident. She asked if I needed a wheelchair. I gladly accepted one. She asked my name and date of birth so she could get me checked in. After she put my information into the computer, she sent me to get an electrocardiogram (EKG). My son asked right away if he could go with me, but he could not because of the severity of my injuries and the limited space in the room. Before they took me away to get the

EKG, my mother arrived just in time to put her eyes on me. She was concerned. It was written all over her face.

When the tech completed the EKG, he pushed me to another station to get an IV so they could administer medicine when I got to my room. The tech told me the dosage the doctor ordered for me was greater than what was typically given to patients. I asked, "Why?" He told me that it may be due to the amount of pain I was in. I felt like it was going to be a long day in the emergency room. After I received the IV, they pushed me into the office to speak to the emergency room doctor.

He shared with me the different tests he ordered and the medicine that would be given to me. I asked the ER doctor why he ordered a higher dosage of medicine for me compared to other patients. He stated it was due to the level of pain he assumed I was in. He offered to reduce the dosage if I was uncomfortable with his recommendation. Frankly, I did not know what I needed. I was in a lot of pain and beat up pretty badly, so I accepted his recommendation. When I left the office with the ER doctor, I was taken to my room. The staff informed my family where I was. My mother and Alijah walked in my room right after. My mother asked me how I was feeling. I told her I was in a lot of pain. She could see the obvious bruises on my hand and leg, but neither one of realized there was so much more.

There were more doctors and nurses that filled my room to get x-rays, administer medicine, and schedule a CT scan. As soon as my mother and Alijah came in my room, they had to go back to the waiting room. There were so many people back and forth. It was not enough room for everyone. I was overwhelmed. Several hours later, all the tests were completed and I was waiting for the results.

Alijah was due at work within a few hours, so I started encouraging him to leave. He would not leave my side. I wanted him to get home in suitable time to take a shower, get dressed, and leave for work before the traffic got too bad. After asking Alijah several times to leave and refusing to do so, my mother reassured him she would be with me until I was discharged. It took numerous pleas for him to leave. He was very reluctant to leave my side, and I understood why. However, I knew he needed the money. After many pleas, Alijah finally left for work.

While I waited for the test results, my mother and I had a transparent conversation. She shared with me the way she felt about different things, and I listened. I wanted her to express her feelings without interruption. It was truly enlightening. Within a few minutes, my mother was in tears and I was fighting back my own. When she stated she could have lost her baby girl in a car accident and was grateful God spared my life, I was filled with so many emotions. Hearing those words out loud did not seem real.

I had never been involved in a car accident before. I took pride in being aware of drivers around me and being a defensive driver. One of the main reasons why I avoided prior accidents was due to my awareness and quick reaction when issues occurred. I was at a loss for words in that moment because I did not know what happened. The last thing I remembered before impact was going through a green light, then BOOM! I never saw the car. I asked God, "Why?" I wanted to know why I never saw the car before impact. I wanted to know why the car pulled out in front of me. I wondered if the driver was distracted. I even wondered if I was distracted. It was the strangest thing I encountered.

A few hours passed and the ER nurse came to provide me with the results of my tests. All the x-rays, CT scan, EKG, and blood work were all normal. There were no signs of any broken bones, fractures, or internal bleeding. I was once again overwhelmed with joy. I was still in a lot of pain, so the doctor administered another round of medicine through my IV. Shortly after, I was discharged. I spent over five hours in the emergency room and was finally going home. God was so good to me. The nurse pushed me in the wheelchair to the parking lot, so my mother could drive me home. I was thankful she had a car because I no longer had transportation.

On the way home, we stopped by CVS to get my prescription filled. Since I was still in a lot of pain, we did not wait for the medicine. I told my mother I would let Alijah pick up the medicine for me. When we got to my house, I was in severe pain. In addition, I was nauseated. The dosage of pain medicine that I received in the emergency room made me sick. My mother stayed with me a little while before she went home. She helped me get undressed because I could not lift my right arm without experiencing excruciating pain. That is when my mother and I discovered a lot more bruises on my body. It was a lot. My arms, chest, stomach, leg, pelvis and hand were all blue. I was very concerned. I was trying to figure out where all the bruises came from. My mother mentioned my seat belt and airbags were probably a major factor. I believed the impact itself was another reason I was beaten up badly. I knew then that I would have a long road of recovery.

After my mom helped me get in the bed, she headed home. I knew Alijah would be home later that evening and I would be okay being home alone for a few hours. Between my dad, siblings, SIS members, friends, and other family members, I had a lot of support. Unfortunately, I still had not heard from DE, and I was starting to worry. I did not know how he would react when he found out I was involved in a very bad accident. I did not want to stress myself out anymore, so I closed my eyes and went to sleep.

Soon after I fell asleep, I woke up again. I felt extremely sick. I wondered why I felt so sick all of a sudden. I had to throw up. Since I was in my room and did not want to create a mess, I slowly pulled myself out of the bed and went into the bathroom. I made it to the bathroom just in time. There was nothing on my stomach because I had not eaten. I assumed the medicine they administered through my IV was too much for me. For several hours I felt nauseated and could not eat. I was afraid that if I did eat something, it would come back up. I was miserable. I drank a few sips of water and went back to sleep.

The next day, I expected to feel worse and experience more soreness but there was no change. Even though the pain did not get worse, it did not get any better. I was no longer nauseous, but I was still reluctant to eat. I knew it would be best to pick up my medicine from CVS as soon as possible. Thankfully, a few months prior I purchased a cash car for Alijah so he could take me to pick up my medicine. He desperately needed a car to get to work and school and I was grateful to be in a position to buy him one. Living in Cobb County meant having a car was a necessity. Now that I no longer had a car, I would need his help getting me back and forth.

After we picked up my medicine from CVS, we went back to the house so I could rest. The day after the accident was the 4th of July, so most places were closed. Therefore, it was no surprise that the police report from the accident was unavailable. My mother came over to spend time with me so I would not be at home by myself when Alijah went to work. The struggles continued. The chest pains were severe. The pain in my neck and arms prevented me from putting clothes on or taking them off without help. The bruises got worse every day. In addition, each day my mother and I found new bruises on my body that we did not see the day before. I was worried.

Even though I picked up my medicine from CVS, it was hard for me to take it consistently. One reason was because I had never been good at taking medicine every day. Another reason was because too much medicine administered in the emergency room caused me to get sick. After several pleas from my family to take medicine, I decided to take a muscle relaxer. It did not help much. It made me sleepy, but I was still in pain. I took ibuprofen, which provided some relief but not much. I started talking to my mother about potential attorneys who could assist with the accident case. She shared with me what she experienced when she was involved in a car accident. I was already overwhelmed.

My mother provided me with the name of her attorney. Since she used them twice, they were at the top of my list. After reaching out to my circle, I had a few additional referrals to choose from. I quickly learned that most accident attorneys request 33 1/3 percent of the proceeds from the case. I was already stressed. It made me wonder if attorneys stopped charging a traditional retainer fee. Or if this was the process for automobile cases only. It was all about the money and that was unfortunate. I learned a few things very quickly regarding this process. I discovered that the amount an accident victim received was based solely on the policy limits. In addition, all medical bills and attorney fees would be deducted from the overall amount.

It was very frustrating. I tried to remain hopeful, but it was hard. After speaking with my mother's attorney, I decided to complete the paperwork with them. The 33 1/3 percent did not sit well with me, so I started to shop around to determine if I could obtain a lower rate. After speaking with a different attorney who was willing to charge me less, I decided that I would retain her business instead. When I reached back out to the attorney who I initially completed paperwork with, they requested I submit a request to terminate representation. I was surprised they requested this. I had just completed the paperwork a few hours ago.

To ensure I covered myself, I did what they requested. The intake coordinator never mentioned this was something I needed to do, so I was surprised. In addition, the case manager was not giving up without a fight. She wanted to know why I decided to leave the firm. I shared with her the rate was too high and I found something lower. She immediately stated that she could potentially match the rate I was offered with a supervisor's approval. She was relentless. I told her I appreciated her efforts but I would like to proceed with terminating representation. She even offered to keep the case active in case I changed my mind. I politely asked her to accept my letter to terminate representation as my final decision. I reassured her that if I changed my mind, I would reach out again to complete new paperwork.

It was very interesting that this was a very popular attorney in Atlanta who had lots of clients. Yet, they were trying so hard to hold on to my case. It felt strange. Then again, several things felt strange because I had never been in this position before. Since the attorney I selected was highly recommended, I decided to take my chances with a smaller firm. She was very personable and professional. The fact that she was willing to reduce my rate made me feel like she was willing to help. Not only did she start off at a lower rate, but she reassured me that if the value of my case was lower than she expected, she would be willing to reduce the rate again. I was very grateful.

My top priority was getting better so I asked my attorney about treatments. She wanted to make things as convenient as possible for me since I did not have a car. Therefore, she located a chiropractor in my area. Once I confirmed the office was close to my home, she told me the office staff would be contacting me soon to set up my initial appointment. The same day, I received a call to schedule my first treatment. Ironically there was availability the same day. Since Alijah did not have to work, he took me to my first treatment and waited for me. I did not know what to expect, but I knew I wanted to do whatever I could to minimize and eventually eliminate the pain I was feeling.

After I completed my paperwork, I was taken back for the first treatment. I started in the massage chair with radiating pads. The pads were placed on my neck and back. This was supposed to help with the pain. Unfortunately, I could not tell much of a difference when the treatment ended. In addition to the massage chair and radiating pads, I saw the chiropractor for an adjustment. I left each treatment feeling the same way I did when I arrived - in pain. Even though the pain I experienced in my neck improved, the chest pains were still problematic.

Since my mother and I found new bruises on my body each day, the attorney recommended I see my gynecologist. Fortunately, within a few days, I was able to get an appointment scheduled. When I arrived for my appointment, I did not know what to expect. The nurse practitioner told me I would have a transvaginal ultrasound done. This is a technique used to examine the uterus, ovaries, tubes, cervix, and pelvic area. There was substantial bruising in my pelvic area, so this procedure was done as a precautionary measure. When the ultrasound was complete, the tech shared with me there were no major concerns. She did not provide a lot of information, because the nurse practitioner was responsible for giving me all the details.

When she came into the room to talk to me, she shared the same results the ultrasound tech shared with me. There were no major concerns, and everything internally looked normal. For that, I was truly grateful. I discovered that a lot of the bruises and injuries I sustained came from the seat belt and airbags. I was shocked by how much damage and protection these things caused. Once I received my prescription, I was free to go. I touched base with the attorney after my gynecologist appointment. She requested all the medical bills I received as a result of the car accident. To make things easier, I signed a medical release so she would receive my records timely.

Weeks passed, treatments continued, but I was still dealing with chest pains. I took ibuprofen as needed every eight hours and iced my chest with the icepack. Nothing seemed to help. My dissatisfaction with my treatment plan was growing. I shared with my attorney that I was not okay racking up unnecessary medical bills that were not helping me get better. She understood and supported me in whatever decisions I made. When I arrived for a scheduled treatment with the chiropractor, I told her the treatments were not helping because I was still in pain, so she sent me to get an MRI. This would provide the images she needed to intelligently assess my chest.

I wondered why the chiropractor did not suggest this when I initially started treatments. Since I knew a few individuals in my circle who dealt with a similar situation, I asked for their feedback. Most of them shared with me though getting the MRI would be helpful, it would be expensive. I was overwhelmed all over again. If I decided to get the MRI, that would be another bill I had to pay. If I refused the MRI, the chiropractor would not be able to adequately treat me. I honestly did not know what I should do. After some time, I declined the MRI. One of the things I liked about the chiropractor is that she was very transparent. She shared with me it would be best for me to cover the MRI out of pocket at $300 or $400 vs placing it against my case. That is because when bills are added as a lien against my case, the price is higher.

I was blown away. Wow! That was how the doctors, and other medical professionals were making their money. They inflated the cost in hopes of being overcompensated. I never wanted to be in this position. I had no intentions of getting rich from an automobile case. Actually, I never planned to be involved in a car accident at all. I was the victim, but everyone had their hands in the pot trying to get a piece of the profit. I was not happy. The information the chiropractor provided allowed me to make a final decision about declining the MRI. I shared with her that I had no intentions of racking up unnecessary bills for the sake of doing so. She understood.

We continued with treatments as planned for a few more weeks. Some days were better than others, but the fact remained I was still dealing with chest pains. My chiropractor suspected I had costochondritis. Costochondritis is inflammation in the cartilage that connects a rib to the breastbone. The description of this condition sounded like the pain I was experiencing in my chest. The projected timeline for this to heal was about six to eight weeks. It was only approaching four weeks since the accident, therefore, I had to allow sufficient time to heal. Sometimes we can be impatient, and I was. I was impatient solely because I had things to do. Dealing with continuous chest pains meant I had to slow down. Thankfully, I did not have a full-time job to clock into each day. It would have created some problems with my employer for sure.

After speaking with my attorney again, I shared with her I was preparing to end treatments since nothing was really helping. The chiropractor encouraged me again to get the MRI done. Despite my initial decline, I told her I would do it. She told me she would reach out to the office that handles MRIs, and they would call me for scheduling. I expected them to call immediately, but they did not. After a few days, I was highly disappointed that no one called me to schedule an appointment.

After a week passed, I told the chiropractor I would not be getting the MRI because no one ever called me to schedule an appointment. I was tired. She sent them an email while I was in the office with her. Even though someone finally called me the same day and everything was scheduled, I called back the next day to cancel. I was over it. Besides, one of my Sista friends in the medical field told me I did not need an MRI to diagnose costochondritis. That was all the confirmation I needed. I sent an email to my attorney letting her know I declined the MRI, and I was done with treatments from the chiropractic. Even though I was still dealing with pain in my chest, I was not okay adding any more bills, especially since the treatments were not helping. I was done. My attorney understood. I consulted with her first to ensure ending treatments would not impact my case negatively. She assured me it would not since previous clients terminated treatments for various reasons.

I moved forward knowing that if I needed any more medical support, I would go to my primary care physician or gynecologist. After I concluded treatments with the chiropractor, I thought the case would be almost over. I was so wrong. My attorney and I usually communicated via email because she was usually in court. If I called her, she answered, but email was the easiest method of communication. However, when I received a call from her one afternoon, I knew something major was happening.

When I answered and we got our greetings out the way, she immediately asked if I had any additional insurance coverages. I did not understand why she asked that question, but I learned quickly. I did not have any other coverages outside of what we had already discussed. If I was the victim, why did I need additional coverage? She received a bill from WellStar for $32,000. My immediate thought was, "What? How? For what?" I was in disbelief.

I wanted to know how WellStar could bill me for $32,000 when I never stayed overnight at the hospital. I never took an ambulance to the emergency room. In addition, nothing was broken so no surgeries were required. I also wanted to know how WellStar could seek legal counsel against me without billing me first. I never received a bill from them besides for the EKG, which I paid immediately. I wanted to know the breakdown of the bill. It was shocking that my attorney received a bill for $32,000 before I ever saw it. The math was not adding up, and I was livid. How could they do this to me? I asked my attorney to send me a copy of all medical bills she received. I needed to see these things in black and white. The fact that WellStar never sent me the bill was quite alarming. I did not know if this was a standard process or if this was just something I experienced. I was not happy.

My attorney shared with me that due to the policy limits for the at-fault driver, having a bill for $32,000 meant that there was already a deficit. The bill from WellStar did not include my attorney fees or the other medical bills. I was very upset. I was angry that WellStar would go through these lengths to get money from me. It was excessive, and I did not like it. I asked my attorney what options were available to me. She told me she would have to negotiate with the insurance company and with WellStar to lower the bill. She explained the process could take up to 60 days. Unfortunately, there was nothing I could do but wait.

Within a few weeks, my attorney was done negotiating with the insurance company. They agreed to pay out the max amount of the insurance policy, which was $25,000. I was pleased with that decision. The next step was to negotiate the medical bills from the chiropractor who my attorney and WellStar sent me to. Sadly, I had other bills I incurred from the accident, but those bills were my sole my responsibility to pay. I was confused, but I learned quickly how things worked. If my attorney sent me to a doctor, they would be paid from the funds she received from the insurance company. If someone placed a lien against my case, which was done by WellStar, they would be paid from the funds from the case as well. Though it was very overwhelming, I was learning a lot. I wondered if an attorney would be necessary if I was involved in a car accident in the future. I wanted to ensure that I did what was in my best interest.

Within a few more weeks, I received a notification regarding another medical bill. I was blown away by the number of bills I received from the car accident. In my opinion, the $32,000 that WellStar billed me should have covered all charges (labs, physician and treatments), but sadly it did not. I forwarded the bill to my attorney so she would know I received another bill. Since the statement did not include my medical insurance, I added my insurance information and sent it back to the medical provider. The frustrating part about the entire process was that WellStar would not allow me to use my health insurance to pay the bill. It was eye opening. They were very greedy and unethical.

My attorney called me shortly after I emailed her a copy of the latest bill. Because the latest bill came from another law office, she wanted to release funds to me to ensure she did not receive any more liens against my file. She sent me a proposed settlement statement. On the statement, WellStar reduced their outrageous bill from $32,000 to $8,333.33. I was still not happy with that amount. I know most would say that it was a good deduction, but in my opinion, it was not. WellStar would not allow me to use my medical insurance to pay the bill. Apparently, according to Georgia law, they were not required to do so, but it did not make it right. Secondly, I did not incur $8,000 in medical expenses in the few hours

I was in the emergency room. Besides, the separate bills that came in addition to the $32,000 were excessive.

I told my attorney that I accepted her recommendation to have funds released to me, but I did not accept the $8,333.33 that WellStar was still trying to bill me for. It was not right. She reassured me she would continue to work on my case, but I was not convinced. On September 18, 2024, I met with my attorney to pick up my check, which was only $7,500. From $25,000, all I received was $7,500. I was angry. I was the victim, but everyone had their hand in the pot. It made me sick to my stomach. It was so wrong. My attorney did reduce her fee by $500, which I was grateful for. It just did not seem fair that I was dealing with this. I was not trying to become rich from the car accident. However, I did not want to have unpaid medical bills remaining when my case was complete. Unpaid medical bills would have negatively impacted my credit, and I did not need that. My attorney shared with me that she would submit another request for a reduction but it would take some time. I understood that everything was a process, and even though I was becoming impatient, I wanted to be fair. I wanted to give my attorney suitable time to work on my behalf. Whenever she had an update for me, she was intentional about communicating timely. On Friday, November 8, 2024, I received an update from my attorney. After several attempts, WellStar provided a final reduction of $7,500. It was a difference of $833.33. Even though I was still unsatisfied with this offer, I accepted it. I was still unemployed so every little bit meant a lot to me. I was tired of going back and forth. I traveled to my attorney's office to pick up the final check. I was grateful for the additional funds, but disappointed that WellStar would not reduce the bill more or allow me to use my medical insurance.

Since my attorney was not in the office when I picked up my final check, I sent her an email thanking her for the services she provided. She was very professional and pleasant, despite my frustrations, so I wanted to convey my gratitude. In addition, I expressed how I was still unsatisfied with the way my case ended. Typically, when I sent correspondences to my attorney, she would respond the same day. This time I did not receive a response, but I did not think much about it.

On November 14, 2024, I woke up to a new Explanation of Benefits (EOB) statement from Aetna, my medical insurance provider. It was alarming because I had not gone to the doctor since the car accident in July. I got out of bed and went into my home office. I turned on my computer and logged into my Aetna account. After reviewing the EOB statement, I realized WellStar finally billed my medical insurance. I was puzzled for a few reasons. One reason was because my attorney shared with me the attorneys for WellStar were unwilling to bill my insurance. Another reason I was puzzled was due to the in-network discount resulting in a substantial reduction to my medical bill. Since I went to an in-network provider, the bill was reduced from $32,000 to $2,227.22. I was shocked and upset. I knew if WellStar was initially willing to allow me to use my medical insurance, my attorney never would have needed to go back and forth with them about reducing the bill. The reality was my attorney was still holding $7,500 for WellStar. I did not know what any of this meant. I calmed down long enough to send my attorney an email expressing how confused and upset I was. Instead of responding to my email, she called me.

Since I expressed my dissatisfaction with how my case was handled, she continued to work with the attorney for WellStar. She asked them to show her in writing where I could not use my medical insurance to cover the bill. In addition, she advised me that since my medical insurance had been billed, that could mean the lien was lifted. If

WellStar lifted the lien from my case, the remaining $7,500 that my attorney was holding would be released to me. Within 24 hours, my attorney sent over a document for me to sign acknowledging that she would be releasing the remaining funds to me, and I would be responsible for paying all medical bills associated with the car accident.

I was grateful for the outcome. I expressed my sincere appreciation to my attorney for her efforts. The funds could not have been released at a better time. God is always, always, showing up for me. He is truly an on-time God. He may not come when we want Him to, but He is truly always right on time. One of the final words from my attorney was, "God truly does not play about you."

CHAPTER 4 LESSON

Throughout this life, we will all encounter obstacles. Some obstacles will be harder than others, but we will get through them. One of my father's favorite lines is "Keep on living." Each day, God blesses us with is an opportunity to keep fighting, keep going, and to never give up. If God brings us to any obstacle, He will bring us through it. We may not get through it as quickly and easily as we hope, but God will help us. We must be willing to seek Him for guidance and trust that He will show us what to do. During this season of my life, I have encountered many obstacles, but I am grateful that God is faithful through it all.

Chapter 5

OBSTACLES TEST: PART II

In this life, we must remember that the enemy comes to kill, steal and destroy. He comes to bring confusion, division and frustrations. It is important to remember that "If God be for us, who can be against us." As previously discussed, in May 2024, I was wrongly released from GS after 10 years of service. Though I was very disappointed, I knew it was essential for me to move forward and prepare for my future. I knew unless I won the lottery, I had to get back to work. I had bills to pay. Most importantly, I needed to rebuild my savings.

In August 2024, I became eligible for unemployment benefits. This was substantial for me because I was still unemployed and every little bit helped. Frankly, until August, I was not actively looking for work. I enjoyed being in the space where I was my own boss. I was also able to spend quality time with my family without restrictions. Plus, there was a waiting period to collect unemployment due to the severance package I received from GS upon my separation. Those resources had to be exhausted first before I could apply. Applying for unemployment benefits in the past was a bit challenging, so I was grateful that the application process and intake interview went smoothly. Within just a short period of time, the counselor determined my eligibility and mailed the approval letter. Even though $365 was not a lot of money, it was the maximum amount I could receive living in the state of Georgia. Getting back to work was essential.

One of the requirements for receiving unemployment in Georgia was attending a workshop at the local unemployment office. When I attended the workshop, my counselor explained that I might be eligible for additional resources. I did not know what that meant, but I wanted to take advantage of any resources I was eligible for. She provided websites that I should use to apply for jobs. She was very helpful and informative. I was hopeful. Another requirement I had to meet to receive unemployment was reporting three job searches each week. The job searches could be applying for a job, posting to a job board, emailing or inquiring about a job with a hiring manager, or attending an interview. This was the first time I took applying for jobs seriously. Even though I was not ready to rejoin the workforce, it was something I had to do. Since my background was education, I decided to finally apply for jobs within the school systems.

Since I live in Cobb County, the school district within my county was ideal. I created a profile, uploaded my résumé and other required documentations, and applied for several jobs. Within a few days, I received calls from different schools asking me to come in for an interview. The first interview, I was hired on the spot as an afterschool instructor. I was grateful for the opportunity because it would allow me to get my foot in the door. As excited as I was for the opportunity, things did not go as planned. Cobb County School District has a rigorous hiring process. The résumé I uploaded to my profile had to match the information I entered on their application. The references had to be current or previous managers. They did not allow other professional or character references. There could not be any gaps in employment, which was standard. I thought I did everything right. The after-school director warned me, but I was not prepared for what came in the weeks following my first job offer.

Each time the request for hire was submitted by the school, the HR department requested more corrections. I went back and forth making corrections for weeks. In the end, once everything was completed, the director went with another candidate. Even though I was disappointed, I understood. Thankfully, I was still filling out applications which resulted in more call from schools to interview. I accepted each opportunity to interview to ensure I could get to work as soon as possible. It was clear that God had other plans. Despite interviewing at 10 different schools and receiving two offers, each offer was rescinded due to the length of time it took to gain approval from HR. Many of the positions I applied for were paraprofessional, after school program teacher, or clerical roles. These were all roles I was qualified to do, but in most cases, I was not selected.

From July until September, I never considered another school district, because I lived in Cobb County. When I kept falling short with Cobb, I decided to apply to other school districts in the state. I remembered being told by my family and friends how teachers were in high demand, so I was hopeful that I would obtain a job. I took a few GACE (Georgia Assessments for the Certification of Educators) exams, ethics training, and completed the substitute teacher training. Sadly, I never heard back from any of those counties. I did not know what I was doing wrong. Instead of applying to public school, I started applying for jobs with community colleges and universities.

I used the resources and websites that the Georgia Department of Labor provided. I reached out to close friends and family members for suggestions. I was becoming desperate. I set up an account with ZipRecruiter, Indeed and CareerBuilder. There were no solid leads. I did learn that applying through companies' websites was best instead of through third-party job boards. I created several résumés. One that catered to educational roles and another that catered to clerical work. I submitted my résumé to a company for review, and it received a high score. When my résumé exceeded one page, I reduced it to one. When my resume seemed too generic, I worked on it until it was better. After revising it multiple times, I started wondering if the reason why I was not getting a favorable response was because of my Doctor of Education degree. Was I overqualified? Was my education intimidating? If my lack of classroom experience was the issue, how would I obtain that experience if no one was willing to give me an opportunity?

It was very disheartening. I was discouraged. I never imagined being a highly educated woman and having major struggles getting back to work. I did not know what I was going to do. I was applying for jobs, but not receiving call backs. I was interviewing, but not being offered the job. I reached out to more individuals in my circle about job opportunities. Most did not have any job leads. When I talked about my experience trying to get back to work, they were surprised. There was a common misconception that because I had four degrees, I would immediately find work. Sadly, that was just not the case. I had struggles like everyone else, despite my education level.

While I desperately struggled to get back to work, I learned from the Georgia Department of Labor that I was considered a dislocated worker. Based on my education level and expertise, it would be challenging for me to get back to work. Since I was considered a dislocate worker, there were additional resources available to me. The Department of Labor provided grants for individuals who wanted to get certifications or those who wanted to return to school to get additional training. I was very intrigued by what this meant for me. I was a 4x degree holder, so returning to school for more training was not ideal, but it was. In 2022, I spoke to my family about wanting to return to school to obtain a paralegal certificate. My passion for law and wanting to help those being taken advantage of fueled that fire within me.

Since I exhausted all my financial aid for school, I was prepared to pay out of pocket for the paralegal program. While I was employed with GS, we received our annual bonuses in March of each year. I knew that would be the perfect time to pay for school. Sadly, when March 2022 arrived, I was not able to pay for school as planned. There were more pressing things to handle. March 2023 and March 2024 came and went, and I was still not able to pay for the paralegal program.

When I was introduced to the grant program with the Department of Labor, I was reminded of the paralegal program that I wanted to enroll in back in 2022. After reviewing the list of certifications, training, and college programs, I discovered the paralegal certificate was an option that would be covered by the Department of Labor. I was so grateful. After I completed the intake process, submitted a lengthy application which required numerous supporting documents, and attended mandatory orientation, I was officially eligible for the Workforce Innovation and Opportunity Act (WIOA) grant through WorkSource Georgia. After a vigorous process, I was approved and enrolled in my first class for the paralegal program. I was very excited to embark on this journey. It was the final piece that I wanted to add to my résumé and by the grace of God, I was able to do so. Thankfully, the program would not consume a large amount of time or take years to complete. I was told if I took two classes at one time, I could finish in 12 months. I was hopeful. I was encouraged. I was ecstatic to conquer yet another goal. While I desperately waited to get back to work, God created this opportunity so I would have something positive to focus on. Not to mention, it was free. God was always looking out for me. He was always making a way, even when I could not see a way.

In my quest to get back to work, I reached out to my favorite cousin Davonne and asked her if she knew anyone hiring. She shared with me that her job was always hiring, and I should check online. When I went online, there were a few positions that were a right fit for me. I was especially intrigued by the client support consultant role. After spending over an hour applying for different roles, I was hopeful. The next day, I continued my search for a new job. I was determined to keep trying until I was offered the right position. Within two days, I received an email to complete an assessment. Upon completion of the assessment, I was invited to complete a video interview.

The next morning, I recorded the video interview and sent it back to the leaders.

While I waited to hear back from the leadership team regarding the video interview, I received a call to interview with a popular university in Atlanta. I was excited for the opportunity to transition into higher education. I was ready to embrace the right opportunity. My interview was scheduled and I prepared myself accordingly. Within a few days, I received an invitation to interview with the managers for the company my favorite cousin worked for. I was ecstatic. Again, in an effort to do well, I prepare myself accordingly.

When I met with the managers for my interview, they asked some really tough questions. Some were associated with my previous role, education and experience. Then there were several questions that asked about my personal goals, accomplishments, and why I decided to apply for a role with their company. I was very transparent, professional, and honest about my responses. They appreciated my transparency. I was surprised that the interview lasted the entire hour that I was scheduled. I left the office feeling encouraged. The following day, I had my panel interview with the university. I did research on the university so I was well prepared. I answered each question clearly and thoroughly. The panel seemed to be impressed with my skills and education. It was encouraging to finally interview with companies who were not intimidated by my education and experience. Within just a few days, I was invited for a second round of interviews for both companies. I was elated to move to the second round of interviews. I was making progress and grateful for the journey.

I completed the second interview with the company my cousin worked for and was encouraged. The interview with the university was scheduled the following week. I knew God had great things in store for me. On October 24, 2024, my son's 23rd birthday, I received my first full time job offer. I was so grateful that the initial email brought me to tears. It was proof that God's timing was always perfect. There was no better way to celebrate my son's birthday than with such good news. The company my cousin worked for was very impressed with my education and experience. It was the first time I felt valued as an educated Black woman with lots of knowledge.

Since I received the job offer from the company I was most interested in working for, I rescinded my application from the university. I thanked them for the opportunity to reach the final round and to be considered for the role. The hiring manager was not happy with the decision, but she wished me well in my new role. Ideally, working for a university would be my dream opportunity. However, the type of work mattered and the pay. I was content with my decision. I knew God would not bring me this far to leave me. After a few weeks of waiting for my information to be verified and my background check to clear, I received my start date. On Monday, November 11, 2024, I resumed full time work with a company that made it clear they valued their employees. My manager was very welcoming and made the onboarding process seamless. I was encouraged that the company valued adequate training. My manager told me I would be in training for two months and would have strong support throughout the process. I was ready to embrace my new journey and extremely grateful that God never failed me.

CHAPTER 5 LESSON

God is so faithful through it all. Through the good, bad, happy, sad, complicated, frustrating, rewarding, and challenging times, he never leaves us. Despite the obstacles this life will bring, we serve a God who never leaves us, nor forsake us. Remember that if God brings you to it, he will bring you through it. Weeping may endure for a night, but joy will come in the morning. Trust God, and watch Him work on your behalf.

Chapter 6
GRIEF TEST

Grief is described as emotional, mental or physical suffering that can be the result of losing a loved one, a job, or the end of a relationship or friendship. While the loss of a loved one is the most common reason an individual experiences grief, the loss of a job and/or partner are also valid reasons to grieve. Losing anything of value could cause emotional, mental or physical suffering, and I have endured my share of pain. Over the last 10+ years of my life, I have encountered many losses. Some were harder to process than others. At times, I did not know how I would make it through. But God...

Grief is a real challenge that many of us face. There is not a one-size fits all for how individuals process grief. Losses do not get better with time. Often, we learn how to deal with the loss a little better, but it does not make it easier.

I had my first major encounter with grief in 2006. On February 1, 2006, I called off work because I was not feeling well. I needed to get better as soon as possible so that I could return to work. Therefore, I decided to take it easy. While I was laying around the house resting, I decided to call my Grandma Perkins. She had recently been released from the hospital, and I wanted to check in to see how she was doing. When I called her, she did not answer. I did not dwell on it too much because usually when she missed my call, she would call me back shortly after. A little time passed and my phone rang. It was a call coming from Grandma Perkins. I was filled with so much joy as I answered the phone. Before the person on the other line could speak, I said "Hey Grandma."

I expected to hear my Grandma Perkins on the other end, but instead it was my mom crying. "Sheirra, something is wrong with your grandma." Hearing those words made my heart drop. My mom was crying so hard my mind could not adequately process what was happening. She asked me to come to the house as soon as possible. During that time, I did not have a car. I was relying on public transportation. Although I was living with Dad and my Bonus Mom and they both had cars, they were at work. I pulled myself together, got dressed, checked the bus schedule, and walked to the bus stop. The knots that formed in my stomach were vast. I was scared. There were so many thoughts going through my mind at that moment. It was hard to process my thoughts over my fear. I was terrified. Honestly, I did not know what to think.

The 115 bus came, and I rode to Glenwood Road. I got off the bus and caught the 107, which would take me to Grandma Perkins' house. Before I made it down Glenwood Road, my mother called me back and told me she was headed to the hospital with Grandma. They would not let her ride in the back of the ambulance with her. That bothered me even more.

I needed to know what was going on, but no one knew. Instead of getting off the bus at my grandmother's house, I rode the bus to the train station and went straight to the hospital.

When I got to Grady Memorial Hospital, I asked the staff where I should go to find her. They were very helpful and told me where to go. As I walked down the hall to find Grandma Perkins and the family, my heart was pounding. The knots in my stomach were tighter. The fear of the unknown was significant. When I walked in the room, I looked around and many of my aunts were there. My sister was also there sitting in a chair. She looked at me and the words that came from her lips were not what I expected to read. She whispered, "Grandma is gone."

With those words, I fell to the floor and everyone in the room rushed to me. I was overwhelmed with sorrow, shock, disbelief, hurt and pain. It was not what I ever imagined. My family members tried to console me, but it did not work. I cried for what seemed like hours. They gave me space and allowed me to cry, and I did. I cried uncontrollably until my cries turned into coughs. My family members once again tried to calm me down because I was making myself sick. I was already sick, which is why I was at home resting. However, I was making myself feel worse. After some time, the nurse came in and asked if we wanted to see her. I was not ready. I could not wrap my head around the fact that my Grandma Perkins was gone. This was the first loss in my family, and it was major. The rock of our family. The glue that held us all together. The Grandma who always got us together despite how it made us feel, was no longer with us. It was such a tough blow to deal with. I was heartbroken. I was sad. I was filled with so many questions. I wanted to know why the doctors allowed her to go home if she was not doing better. I wanted to know why God took her away from us. My heart was shattered.

When we walked into the room to see her before they released her to the funeral home, the emotions took over me. To see her laying in the bed lifeless was devastating. I was ready for the nightmare to end. Once we concluded our time with her, we all went back to Auntie Betty's house. I stayed with my auntie for a few days. It helped being around family members, but the loss was substantial and it was hard processing it all. It was hard to sleep the days leading up to her funeral. I was dealing with so much sorrow. My heart was broken. I wondered how I would make it without my grandma, but God knew.

The funeral came and went. I cried, cried and cried some more. I was still in shock. I thought talking to family members would help, but it did not. I thought being around my family would help, but it only lasted for little while before I was sad all over again. The reality was, Grandma Perkins was gone, and she was not coming back. In December 2005, she had an 80th birthday celebration. I recall her saying, "I am so glad to have all my family here with me. This is my last birthday." In that moment, I thought she was just saying it would be the last time she would have a birthday party. I never imagined she was letting us know it would be her final birthday here on earth. The thought of her words was gut-punching. I never imagined two short months after her 80th Birthday celebration she would no longer be here with us. Though this loss was major, I was grateful to God for allowing me to have such an amazing grandma in my life. She meant the world to me, and I showed her in my actions while she was still here.

Sadly, the loss of Grandma Perkins was the first of many to follow. A short time after she passed away, we lost one of my cousins. It was another tough blow. None of us ever imagined we would experience another loss so quickly after my grandma. After laying my cousin to rest, we dealt with another loss when one of my uncles passed away. He was riding his bike home, and someone hit him but never stopped to help him. After several days in ICU, my uncle passed away from the injuries he sustained from the hit and run accident.

From a spiritual perspective, I understand we will all leave this life behind one day. Ultimately it is a part of life. No one will live forever. We are taught this all our lives. However, seeing my loved ones pass away has been very difficult to process. Especially when some losses were back-to-back.

In 2013, as I was preparing to obtain my associate degree, Grandma Dean became very ill. She was my father's mother. Most days it was hard to focus on school because I was concerned about my grandma. She rarely got sick and when she did it was usually just a cold. She had a history of losing her voice often, but besides that she was healthy. Or, at least that is what we thought. Grandma Dean did not go to the doctor regularly. She put her trust in God for complete healing. So, if anything needed to be addressed, we did not know.

When Grandma Dean got sick and had to remain in the hospital, I went to see her every chance I got. Between school and work, it was not always easy, but I made a way. I wanted to be there. I needed to be there. Not just for her, but for Daddy who I knew was dealing with a lot. Grandma Dean had to have surgery, and we hoped that would help her get better. However, as time went on, Grandma became very weak. I could not recall a time when she could not take care of herself, but during that time, she needed a lot of support. Thankfully, she had all of us, especially Grandfather Dean and Daddy to help her. After some time, Grandma Dean was discharged from the hospital. We were all relieved. I never knew what surgery she had or what was going on with her medically, but I was grateful she was able to leave the hospital and go home. Even though Grandma was very weak, we thanked God she was no longer in the hospital.

In May 2013, I obtained my first degree, and Grandma Dean was extremely proud of me. She said, "I do not know why it took so long, but I am glad to know you finished." In 2003, I lost my financial aid and had to withdraw from school. I was a single mom, taking care of my son, and paying all the household bills by myself. Therefore, paying for school out of pocket was not an option for me. This was something Grandma did not know. She was not aware of the circumstances I faced to obtain my first degree. I never had an opportunity to tell her. However, her saying she was proud of me made me happy. I always wanted to make my family proud.

Shortly after I obtained my first degree, I started working on my bachelor's degree at Kennesaw State University. I shared with Grandma Dean that I was enrolled in school again. It was her words that encouraged me. She said, "Sheirra, do not stop. Keep going." Her words and my passion to get done with school was all the ammunition I needed to keep moving forward.

Sadly, not long after I started my second semester at KSU, Grandma's condition got worse. She never missed church, but during her time of illness, she regularly missed service. Sometimes, we would take turns staying with her. Other times, she would tell us to go to church. I was still juggling a busy schedule with work, school, and taking care of Alijah, but it was important to show up for Grandma Dean whenever she needed me. One Saturday evening, I decided to stop by her house and check on her. I truly found value in spending time with my family. This time was no different. I wanted Grandma to know she was loved and supported through it all. During our visit, Grandma was very emotional. She mentioned that she was tired. My Grandma Dean was not eating much, and things were moving in slow motion. I was concerned, but grateful to spend time with her. Despite how I felt, I remained strong for her. Before I left to go home, Daddy arrived to offer his. I gave her a hug and told her I loved her. That was the last time I saw Grandma Dean alive.

On Sunday, November 10, 2013, my family and I were at church like normal. Grandma asked Grandfather Dean to go ahead to church so we did not have to cancel service. Since my grandfather was the pastor, my grandma understood the importance of him being in church. This was one of the first times I recalled Grandma Dean being at home alone. Since the church and their home were close, we did not worry too much about her being there alone. After church, I drove home to cook dinner for

Alijah and me. I had homework to do that I knew I would work on when I was done cooking. While I was cooking, I received a call from my lil sis, Celena. When I answered, she immediately said, "You must have not talked to your Daddy?" I said, "No, what is going on?" I was not expecting for her to say what she said next.

Celena shared with me that when Grandfather Dean got home from church, Grandma Dean was unresponsive. I was in total shock. I had so many questions that she did not have the answers to. I could not imagine what my grandfather went through seeing Grandma unresponsive when he got home. He held it together long enough to reach Daddy. Since everyone was on their way home, my parents got to my grandma's house pretty quickly. While Celena was still on the phone, I told her I was going to turn the food off and head to the hospital.

Alijah and I got in the car and headed to the hospital. Unsure which hospital they were taking Grandma Dean to, I had to reach out to my family to get that information. I learned with my Grandma Perkins that despite her going to Atlanta Medical for all her medical care, during an emergency situation, the paramedics will transport patients to the closest hospital. Grandma Dean was transported to Dekalb Medical Hospital. There were so many thoughts running through my mind. Was she going to be okay? Are the medical professionals taking care of her the way they should? How were my grandfather and my daddy handling this? Despite the thoughts, fear, and worry, Alijah and I arrived at the hospital safely.

I spoke to my grandfather who was very hopeful. He him said to us, "I strongly believe this is what she needed to get better." Hours passed and we had not heard anything about Grandma Dean. We were in the lobby talking and trying not to worry. My bonus mom, Momma K, took Alijah and me to get food. When we got back to the hospital, there were no new updates. All we knew was that they were still working on her. I did not know what that meant, but that was the only information they gave us.

It was getting late, and Alijah had to go to school the next morning. I had work and school, but I was committed to being there for my family during this time. There were so many things that were not clear, but we stuck together through it all. After some time had passed, Momma K encouraged me to get Alijah home so he could rest and prepare for school. I agreed that for nothing else,

I needed to get him home so he could go to bed at a decent time. Sadly, hours passed and we still did not know how Grandma Dean was doing. I did not feel like leaving my family, but I left so Alijah could rest. When I got home, I tried to focus on other things, but it was tough. Alijah ate some of the food I cooked before we left home, took a bath, and climbed in the bed.

As for me, I tried to focus on my school, but it was very hard to focus. Later that night, I texted my Daddy to obtain an update on Grandma Dean. A few moments later, I received a message that crushed my heart, "Your Grandma Dean passed away at 10:30 p.m." I was devastated. I was heartbroken. I cried for what seemed like hours, but it was merely only minutes. I held it together long enough to email my professors to let them I would not be able to attend class that week, due to death in my family.

It was a lot to process. I wanted to know what happened and why Grandma Dean was no longer here with us. I asked God, "Why?" I wanted to know why God did not heal her. Nothing made sense. The emotions that I felt were overwhelming. I was sad. I was hurt. I was heartbroken. I was upset. I was disappointed. I felt confused. I felt robbed of an opportunity to say goodbye when I left the hospital.

Not to mention, I knew the pain for my grandfather and father were vast. My grandfather was convinced Grandma Dean would get better, and unfortunately, she did not. I knew that was gut-punching for him. Daddy was dealing with the reality that for the first time in his life, he no longer had his mother. I knew that was devastating for him. It was a new norm he was forced to face. It was a new norm that all of us were forced to face. She was more than a mother, wife, grandmother, great grandmother, auntie or sister. She was the First Lady of our church, she played the organ and helped others learn to play it as well. Grandma Dean was a loyal friend, God mother, and a prayer warrior. She was over the women's work in our church and so much more. If it was hard for me to focus and sleep, I knew it was hard for everyone.

The next few days were a whirlwind of emotions - from spending time with my family to being present for the planning of the funeral. It seemed so unreal. When I lost Grandma Perkins in 2006, I never imagined seven short years later I would lose Grandma Dean, too. It was so hard to process my emotions. Being close to both of my grandmothers made their transition very tough for me. There was nothing that my grandmothers would not do for me. I reciprocated those efforts as an adult. I made sure they knew while they were here with me that I appreciated everything they did for me. Not only did my grandmothers do a lot for me, but they also showed the same love and support to Alijah as well. I was so grateful for the time I was able to spend with them.

Since I knew the loss of my Grandma Dean was very difficult for Daddy, I wanted to support him unconditionally during that time. Daddy talked to Grandma Dean every single day. I do not recall a time when they did not talk to one another every day. The fact that he no longer had that option was hard. I knew I could not fill the void of him not being able to talk to my grandmother, but I could do something. I decided that we would have a Daddy-Daughter Day each week. This was something we never did before, but it was important for me to try something new. I felt it would provide the perfect opportunity to check in with one another just to see how things were going. Some weeks we checked in just to say hello or I love you. That meant a lot to me, so I knew it meant more to Daddy.

After we laid Grandma Dean to rest, the reality set in that she was really gone. It was so difficult trying to process it all. The comfort I held on to was that she was no longer suffering. She was no longer in pain. She was no longer weak and fragile. Though those thoughts did bring some comfort, most days it was not enough. I was moving through the motions of yet another loss. I knew without a doubt it would take some time to get through. This was just the beginning of a new norm.

In 2017, four years after Grandma Dean transitioned, my grandfather passed away. It was another tough blow for my family. I was at work and did not expect the call that came from Momma K. It was such a heartbreaking moment for me. Daddy went to my grandfather's house for his daily visit and found him unresponsive. The tough reality was that the way Daddy found my grandfather was the same way my grandfather found Grandma Dean, his beloved wife. Though the paramedics were able to resuscitate Grandma Dean before transporting her to the hospital, that was not the case for my grandfather. It was too late. He was gone.

Thankfully, when I received the news, I did not have to stay at work. My manager told me I could leave for the day and to let her know what I needed. I was not prepared mentally for another loss. My first thought was of Daddy who was now grieving the loss of both of his parents. Since I could not recall Daddy fully grieving the loss of my Grandma Dean, I knew this would be difficult. Besides, this loss was unexpected.

Shortly after Grandma Dean passed away, my grandfather's health began to decline. He lost his eyesight and was no longer able to drive. Despite the decline in his health, he still attended church and preached his weekly message. None of us imagined he would be gone shortly after Grandma Dean. Who would lead us now that my grandfather was gone? There were no other pastors in our church. But God. He always makes a way, even when we cannot see a way. Our Bishop in London was the individual who agreed to call us each week and provide the message over the phone. It was such a blessing. The church was different. We no longer had the founders with us, and we were not prepared for church without them. Thankfully, Daddy was determined to see the church move forward, and so it did.

Two short weeks after we laid my grandfather to rest and attempted to resume normalcy, I logged into Facebook to several posts telling my best friend since 7th grade to rest in peace. I was confused. I was in disbelief.

I was wondering why there were so many posts about my best friend, but I had not heard anything from the family yet. I immediately sent a message to my best friend's brother. I asked him to please tell me my best friend was okay and the posts that I saw on my timeline were not accurate. Sadly, he confirmed that the posts were valid, and she was no longer with us. I broke down immediately. I was hurt. I was overwhelmed. I was once again devastated. It was only 14 days or less since we lost my grandfather, but I was faced with yet another loss. My God! I just did not have the words to say.

In that moment, all I could do was weep. I gathered my thoughts long enough to ask what happened. I never imagined I would receive the words that came from my best friend's brother. He told me she committed suicide. I was in disbelief all over again. I wanted to know why. I wanted to know what caused the desperation. We were left with so many unanswered questions. Her brother told me she spoke to someone the day before she took her life and that individual missed the warning signs. Or that individual simply did not take her cry for help seriously. This news was hard to process. After going back and forth with her brother for a little while, I logged off social media. It was too much to deal with.

The news of my best friend committing suicide was heartbreaking. It made me feel sad knowing she did not remember to call me when she was going through life challenges. She was living in Ohio, but we kept in touch as much as our schedules allowed. Often, I asked myself if there was anything I could have done to help her. In that moment, I knew I would never know.

Her mother traveled from Atlanta to help prepare and plan the service. I knew, as a mother, she never anticipated having to bury her child. I know the pain was substantial for her. It was such a sad time for all of us. I never imagined being in this space of losing one of my best friends to suicide. My feelings and emotions were all over the place.

Sadly, I was unable to say my final goodbye because I was in Atlanta. My best friend was laid to rest in Ohio because that was home for her. Although she lived in Atlanta for many years, she moved back to Ohio when she got home from the Army. In most cases, home is where we long to be. We gravitate more to the places we consider home. However, it was evident that though my best friend was home, it was not a happy place for her. Since I could not make it to Ohio, her brother promised he would save an obituary for me. He did just that. It was put together well and represented my best friend beautifully.

The truth remained, I was mentally drained. There was so much happening at one time. Before I had adequate time to grieve one family member or friend, I was faced with the loss of someone else. I needed strength to endure. Sadly, two short months after my best friend was laid to rest, her mom passed away as well. My auntie on my daddy's side of the family passed away right after. Not to mentioned I learned that another childhood best friend lost her mom, too. I became numb. I could no longer process my feelings adequately. I needed support. I reached out to my company's Employee Assistance Program (EAP) to explore available options. I learned quickly that I could speak with a mental health therapist with no out-of-pocket cost. The company covered up to six sessions per year, and I felt that was a good start.

I was matched with a therapist who was close to my home which was convenient. However, it was not effective. After a few sessions, I determine the therapist was not a good fit for me. I needed someone who was relatable and could cater more to my demographic as an African American female. Therefore, I concluded after two sessions. I was not in the mental space to explore other options, so I did not resume therapy.

In 2021 after experiencing several challenges with my manager at work, I decided it was time to explore new options for therapy. I understood early that therapy was not just for those dealing with grief. Therapy is designed to support all aspects of our lives. Although I was not dealing with grief, I was dealing with work conflicts, and I needed support on how to adequately handle the occurrences. Thankfully, I found a great therapist who was knowledgeable, relatable, professional, caring and understanding. Not to mention she was encouraging, supportive, and very resourceful. I was extremely grateful for our connection. Things went so well with my therapist that after I used my company-paid sessions, I used my insurance or paid cash to continue monthly sessions. She provided valuable tools, suggestions and resources that helped me redirect my energy when I felt overwhelmed. I finally felt like I had someone outside my family to offer adequate support.

Many of my family members did not know I spoke to a therapist. Some of them were surprised when they found out, while others were very supportive. Seeing a therapist in the African American community it not a popular choice. However, it was important to do what was best for me. I was willing to do whatever it took to maintain a healthy mental space. The media talks a lot about mental illness when someone is involved in mass shootings. Yet, we do not talk about the things that we can do to prevent mental illness from becoming a major problem.

It did not matter who did not agree with my decision to see a therapist. I was intentional about taking care of me. It was essential to have a strong support team during times when I needed guidance and direction the most. Therefore, I did what I had to do. In January 2025, I received new insurance benefits since I was with a new company. Unfortunately, my therapist was not covered under the new insurance. Since I was not ready to start this journey with someone new, I moved to a cash-pay client instead.

In addition to the health and wellness incentives we received with my new company, I also gained access to a wellness coach. I was very impressed with the wellness coach I was assigned. She provided helpful tools and resources that were beneficial as well. I was grateful for the additional support. God knew I would need it.

In September 2024, I received word from my mom that my auntie was being moved to hospice care. My auntie was dealing with Stage IV cancer. It spread to vital parts of her organs, and there was nothing more the doctors could do. I was in disbelief. I felt like I was on a roller coaster ride, and I desperately wanted to get off. Even in that moment, I knew my God was bigger. I knew he had the final say. I knew he was able to do exceedingly abundantly above what we could ask or think. I was grateful I did not have a full-time job to run to every day. It allowed me to spend a lot of time with my auntie. I went to see her two or three times a week while she was in the hospital. I went to see her every other day when she moved to hospice care.

Each time I went to see her she knew who I was. With the exception of the first day I went to see her in the hospital, she was in good spirits despite what she faced. The first day I visited her, she was a bit down. She expressed to me that she did not like having to depend on others to do things for her. She was very sad. During that time, I asked her if I could pray with her. She agreed. As I looked to God for the words to say, I said a prayer over my auntie that I knew would be beneficial. It gave me peace, and a calmness filled my auntie's eyes. I was overjoyed that I could encourage her in that moment.

From the hospital to hospice care, I wanted to be there with my auntie during this very tough time. When she asked me to bring her something, I made sure I did just that. One day, she asked me to bring her some cookies on my next visit, but when I went back, I forgot the cookies. My auntie did not let me forget her cookies again because she talked about them the entire time I was with her! The next time I went to see her, I made sure I had those cookies.

The doctors at the hospital told my cousin that my auntie only had a few days to live. When I say God is in control, He is in complete control! In March 2025, after six months in hospice care and fighting to the very end, my auntie transitioned. Though the news of her passing was hard, I was grateful for the opportunity to spend a lot of time with her. I logged off work for the day and drove to the hospice care facility to see her one final time. My auntie wanted to be cremated, so I knew this would be my last opportunity. When my cousin arrived, we walked into my auntie's room and said our final goodbyes. She looked like she was just sleeping. She looked like she was at peace, and for that I was extremely grateful. The hospice facility had a brief service for her outside, and the crematory facility drove her body away immediately following. It was the last time I saw my auntie. I was sad, but the goodness of God made me feel better. I spent a lot of time with her before she passed, so that made me feel good.

I had a lot to unpack when I met with my therapist in April 2025. Not only was I dealing with the loss of another family member, but there were challenges within my home as well. She supported me through it all. She listened as I shared the things I endured since our last meeting. She reminded me that I needed to take care of myself first. She provided additional resources that I could use to handle grief. Every little bit helped, and it was necessary. I was willing to do whatever I needed to do to ensure my mental space was healthy.

In June 2025, I received more devastating news regarding a close family member. My cousin, who was like a mom to me and a grandmother to my son, was diagnosed with Stage IV cancer. I was shocked when I received the news. It did not seem fair that cancer was attacking members of my family at an alarming rate. I was mentally drained. I did not understand why we were dealing with so much heartache and pain. It was a tough time for my family again. I desperately needed God to have mercy. This was extremely difficult because my cousin was in Atlanta in May watching her daughter get married. She was in good spirits and celebrating such a joyous moment in her daughter's life. It seemed unreal that only a month later, we were faced with such gut-punching news.

I wanted to know why, so I questioned God. I asked questions that I knew I would not get the answers to right away, but I was sure God would reveal things in his timing. Things moved much quicker with my cousin than they did with my auntie. It was difficult for me to spend time with her because she lived in California. The thought of losing another family member was pulling at my heartstrings. I prayed hard that treatment would work and my cousin would have a full recovery. Sadly, things did not work out the way I prayed they would. The tough reality that we faced was that my cousin never started treatment. She had numerous seizures back-to-back, which meant she was not strong enough to undergo treatment. After a few short weeks, we received word that there was nothing else the doctors could do. I was heartbroken. I was devastated. I was worried about how my son would handle this news. It was too much to deal with at one time. The continuous loss was disheartening. The pain was unbearable. My heart was broken. It was a lot to process.

On Sunday, August 31, I woke up to the news that my cousin had passed away. As the tears fell from my eyes, I had difficulty breathing. I tried hard to keep myself calm, but it was impossible. My son was at work, so I did not have to hide my emptions. I immediately sent prayers and love to my favorite cousin. I knew this was extremely difficult for her and my auntie. I never imagined just five short months later, we would experience another loss. I needed more strength to endure.

While my favorite cousin and auntie were in California finalizing my cousin's affairs, we received more devastating news that another family member passed away. I was officially numb. I was at a loss for words. I asked God to please show us what we were doing wrong to continue to endure the level of pain we were dealing with back-to-back. I needed substantial support, so I reached out to my therapist to schedule a session. I also reached out to my wellness coach to let her know the things I was dealing with as well.

My wellness coach responded immediately and offered support. Surprisingly, though, I was not able to schedule a session with my therapist. She never accepted the appointment nor sent me the link for a virtual session. That was unlike her, so I was worried. When the day and time came for our session, she was a no-show. I sent emails and text messages, but I never received a response. I prayed that she was doing well, but I just did not know. After weeks of not hearing back from my therapist, I started looking for a new one. I needed support more than ever. After looking into the Employee Assistance Program (EAP) with my current job, I realized I was entitled to eight sessions per occurrence. Therefore, I started looking for a new therapist who would be the right fit for me.

With everything going on in my family, I was not ashamed to admit I needed help. I was not okay, and I needed all the support I could get. Not to mention, I still needed to tell my son about my cousin passing away. I knew he would not take it well. She was a major part of his life growing up. She helped potty train him and enrolled him in his first Pre-K program. She took him to work with her when I was working, so he spent a lot of time with her. This conversation would not be easy.

One morning when I was walking out the door to go to the dentist, I decided it was time to give Alijah the news. As expected, he was heartbroken. His expression said exactly what I expected it to. This was difficult for him and I needed him to process his emotions effectively. I recommended he speak to someone to help him process his emotions. I reminded him of all the things she encouraged him to do and not to do when he was growing up. I needed him to understand he had to keep on living and make her proud.

I realize that death is a part of life, which means I will experience grief. Therefore, it is critical to adequately process grief when I am faced with these occurrences. I am confident God will give me the strength to endure no matter how tough life gets. He may not provide me with all the answers immediately, but I know He will. I am at peace knowing that if God brings me to it, He will bring me through it. My loved ones who have transitioned meant the world to me while they were here. I know they will hold a place in my heart for years to come. My Grandma Perkins, Grandma Dean, Granddaddy Dean, my best friend, uncles, aunties, and cousins will remain forever in my heart.

CHAPTER 6 LESSON

Grief is a painful and emotional response to a significant loss. There is not a one-size fits all for how we process grief. Some people handle grief quickly. While others take months or years to fully overcome. Regardless to the length of time it takes you to process grief, do so on your own terms. Do not be afraid to decide what works best for you. Remember, God will not put more on us than we can bear. Be encouraged, even during difficult times. God got us through the good, bad, happy, and sad times.

OBEDIENCE

Chapter 7

OVERCOMING TEST

To overcome means to succeed after dealing with a challenge. It could be something as simple as passing a math test after not having success previously. Or it could be something as major as conquering a fear of flying by taking the first flight. Another definition for overcome is to get the best of something. Personally, for me overcoming means to conquer or defeat obstacles. As previously mentioned, we have all encountered obstacles throughout this life. These things are inevitable. However, how we conquer those obstacles will depend on several factors. In my case, the way I have conquered my obstacles have solely been based on my spiritual relationship with God. He is truly the reason I am an overcomer. I ran across a post on social media that resonated with me so much. It stated, "Surrender does not mean giving up, it means giving in." Sometimes all it takes for us to overcome, is to fully give in and trust God.

For the first time in nine years, I did not have a car to call my own. Although this was major, it was not something I thought much about. My biggest focus was getting better physically. I spent so much time trying to eliminate the pain I experienced from the car accident, that I had not considered the mental trauma I was going through. I was headed to the hair salon for the first time since the car accident. I did not consider how attempting to make that trip again would impact me, but I found out quickly. When Siri announced I should take exit two onto Washington Road, my heart started beating very fast. The chest pains were severe. I was grasping for air. I could hardly breathe. I passed the exit and went to Old National Highway instead. Until that moment, I never considered how making a trip to the hair salon would make me feel. When I finally arrived, I realized I had a severe anxiety attack.

Sadly, that was not the only time I experienced an anxiety attack after the car accident. I was on higher alert because I did not want to be involved in another car accident. Whether I was running quick errands, attending church, or tutoring my kids, the anxiety I felt in those moments was often substantial. For several weeks straight when I went to the hair salon, it resulted in an anxiety attack. Each instance was different. They ranged from severe, moderate or mild. Each time the navigation asked me to get off on Washington Road, I went around to Old National Highway instead. I could not bring myself to take the same route I was attempting to take when I was involved in the car accident. I knew it would take some time. I was not ready to conquer that fear.

Thankfully, I was still meeting with my therapist each month to ensure I maintained a healthy mental space. When I still worked for GS, I found value in utilizing the resources they provided. The EAP was one of the resources I used every year. EAP was how I connected with my therapist. In 2021 when I was dealing with substantial stress with my manager, I needed a safe space to make my voice heard and to obtain an effective approach for handling the stress. I was very grateful when Mutual of Omaha provided my therapist information to schedule my initial session. From the first session in 2021 until now, she has been professional, pleasant and personable.

Maintaining regular sessions helped me unpack the good, bad, happy, sad, frustrating and rewarding things happening in my life. My therapist has always been very supportive and resourceful. It has been a great fit from the start. When we met a few days after the car accident, she acknowledged that I went through a traumatic event. She was grateful that I was still alive, given the severity of the accident. We talked through some things which required reflecting on what happened the day of the accident. She provided healthy tips, tools and suggestions to ensure I could process the trauma effectively. I understood there was a long journey ahead, but I was willing to do the work to restore my peace.

Once I began my journey to restoring my peace and minimizing the anxiety, I knew I needed to handle other challenges as well. The fact remained, I no longer had a car to call my own. Since my mother and son had cars, I knew if I needed a ride, I could depend on one of them. If they were unavailable, I knew I could take an Uber. Not having my own car was not something I dwelled on much. I knew eventually I would need reliable transportation, but I did not know how I would conquer this task. While my attorney and I waited for the police report to become available, she suggested I file the damages with my insurance company. I was very hesitant to take this approach because I did not know how filing the claim would impact future premiums. I wanted to minimize my cost by any means necessary. My attorney suggested filing a claim with my insurance company because she assumed I had rental car coverage.

I did not. Therefore, I would not be able to get a car as quickly as she thought I would. Thankfully, because

I was not working a full-time job that required me to commute to the office, a car was not needed immediately. However, I would need a car when I resumed in-person tutoring sessions, which were set to start again in August 2024. After I filed the claim with Progressive, I was assigned a claims representative. The claims representative was the point of contact for all things related to my car damages. When I mentioned I had an attorney, she told me she would no longer be able to talk to me. My attorney provided authorization to the claims representative to talk to me regarding the damages only. My attorney cautioned me regarding what I should discuss with the claims representative. Therefore, I kept our conversations brief and was very mindful of the information I shared.

The claims representative shared that I needed to have my car moved from the tow yard by July 11th because Progressive would no longer pay for charges beyond that date. I wondered how I was supposed to move a car that was inoperable. I was told by my claims representative that I could not use my roadside assistance to have it towed. I could sign a release, and Progressive would have the car moved to one of their facilities. On Friday, July 5th, I attempted to rent a car so I could run errands in preparation for my organization's Family & Fun Day. When I arrived at Hertz, I realized the car I reserved through Uber was not available. Though Hertz did have cars available, they were SUVs, which cost more money. I was not prepared to drive a big car. Neither was I prepared to pay more than I planned.

I did not want to inconvenience my mother or rely on Alijah's help, so I wanted to get the rental car. Frankly, I was not sure if I was ready to be behind the wheel again two days after the car accident. Since my mother had already offered to take me where I needed to go, I called her to let her know what was going on. My mother reiterated I could have just called her, and she would have taken me where I needed to go. So, I took an Uber back home and waited for her to pick me up.

Within a few hours, my mother picked me up and took me to the tow yard to remove my specialty license plate from the car. It was the only thing Alijah did not remove when he gathered everything else from the crash site. As I looked at my car, I was very emotional. Tears began to roll down my face. I still could not believe I survived such a bad car accident. My car was totaled, but it had not been officially confirmed yet. I just knew based on how badly the car was damaged. I was overwhelmed with gratitude for still being alive. I was overwhelmed with sadness because I was almost done paying my car off, and it was now gone.

Whew, I was filled with so many emotions in that moment. I took pictures of White Diamond and said my final goodbyes. White Diamond was the name I gave my car on July 23, 2020, when I purchased it in Charlotte, North Carolina. I had no major issues with the car, and it was the newest car I had purchased. I took care of White Diamond by ensuring she received routine maintenance in a timely manner. I did not want to be stuck on the side of the road because I failed to do those things necessary to ensure she ran properly. As my mother drove me home, I reflected on all the road trips, events, games, jobs, and the errands I was able to execute because I had a reliable car. I was grateful.

On July 8, 2024, I spoke to my claims representative again about having the car picked up from the tow yard. As we prepared to plan for release and pick-up of the car, she inquired about the set of keys for the car. I told her there was only one set of keys. Then she asked me where the keys were. I shared with her that the keys were with me on my keyring. When she told me the keys needed to be with the car for pick up, I was upset. If the keys needed to be with the car, why was I just being told this. The tow truck driver never asked for them when I was leaving the crash site. I went to the tow yard previously to get my license plate and could have left the key then, if someone told me I needed to do so. I was frustrated and my claims representative knew it. She told me they would pick up the car the next day. Therefore, I had to figure out a way to get back to the tow yard to drop off the keys.

Later that afternoon, I was communicating with one of my close sista friends, AR. She invited me to come spend time with her in the pool. As much as I was dealing with, I really needed some water therapy. It was so calming and relaxing. Unfortunately, I did not have a car to get around like I wanted to, so I explained this her. Shortly after, she told me she had a car I could use. She followed up by saying the car was not a lot, but I could use it if I wanted to. I was overwhelmed with joy. I asked, "Are you serious?" You have a car that I can use?" She responded "Yes, I have a car you can use. I will take it to get an emissions test. When that is done, I will go get the tag. All you will need to do is get insurance." I was in disbelief, but so grateful.

AR took the car to get the emissions test. After I added the car to my insurance policy, the tag office issued a license plate. Things fell into place quickly and efficiently. AR said she would pick me up the next day to get the car, and that is what she did. She picked me up from home and we went back to her house. She gave me necessary information regarding the car, and I was on my way. God always knows how to make a way when we cannot see a way. I never imagined someone in my circle being willing and able to offer me a car to drive with no stipulations. It was truly a testament to the authentic people I have in my circle. After I picked up the car, I drove straight to the tow yard to release the keys. When I got home, I called my claims representative to let her know the keys were with the car. She thanked me for getting the keys dropped off so quickly.

Later that day, my claims representative called to let me know the car had been picked up and they had completed the devaluation process for my car. My car was deemed a total loss, which I figured it would be. Even though I knew the car was a total loss, getting the confirmation made it a little hard for me. The next step was determining how much my car was worth or figuring out how much Progressive would give me. A few days prior, I went on the website for Kelly Bluebook to determine what my car was worth. It had less than 70K miles and was in pretty good condition prior to the accident. According to Kelly Bluebook, my car was worth about $8k-$12K. Since I only owed $6,749.51 for my car, I was hoping Progressive would have at least offered that so I could pay my car off. One thing I knew for sure was that God would do exceedingly abundantly above what we could ask or think.

I knew insurance companies used their own system for determining a car's value, so I was not sure what Progressive would offer me. I was prepared to move forward with whatever the offer was. When my claims representative told me Progressive was prepared to settle for $14,241.94, I was in total shock and amazement. The offer was also the full total after my $500 deductible. I was so surprised with the offer, I asked her to repeat it again. When she repeated the total and I paused again, she was nervous.

She said she could not tell if I was upset or okay. I let her know that I was extremely grateful for the offer and needed to know what was next. She burst out in laughter, which I knew was a relief for her. She mentioned in a lot of cases, the customers are upset with the offer. I reassured her I was satisfied with the offer and happy. She told me the next steps included going into a Progressive service center to sign the power of attorney. Then, they would need an ownership release from the lien holder, confirming they would release the title to Progressive upon receipt of the payment. Once all necessary documents were received, Progressive would release payment.

The next day, I had an appointment scheduled at 9:45 a.m. to sign the paperwork for Progressive. Since I would receive a payment to me directly for $7,492.43, it created an opportunity to get another car. I never imagined being in a position where my previous car would be paid off in full and feasible resources to get something else. I was thankful. I did not know how I would get another car, but I knew I would have available funds. I started considering financing through Capital One since I had a car loan with them previously. They believed in giving consumers another chance, so I felt my chances with them were good.

Since Prestige Financial approved me in 2020, a month after my bankruptcy was discharged, I figured they could finance a new car loan as well. Besides, I had great payment history for four years, and that should count for something. My only concern with Prestige Financial was the interest rate. When I got my first car, my interest rate started at 17.99 percent. For every three months I made on-time payments and kept my personal information updated, I received a .25 percent interest rate deduction. My interest rate before my car was totaled was about 15.50 percent. I felt it was possible for me to get a lower interest rate since it was four years since my bankruptcy was discharged.

My last option was Navy Federal Credit Union. I have been a member with Navy Federal since 2007. Though our banking relationship has not always been good, I attempted to rebuild our fragile bond. It seemed no matter what I tried to do, Navy Federal would not approve me for any of their products and services. I applied for credit cards, but I was denied. I applied for the secured credit card and was initially denied. After some time passed, I applied again and was approved. However, several years later, I have not been offered a regular card or a credit line increase. I always wanted the opportunity to get a credit card with Navy Federal because they had high credit limits and low interest rates, but I was never successful. Therefore, when I received an email from Navy Federal regarding a car loan, I was in denial. I felt if they would not approve me for a credit card, there was no way they would approve me for a car loan. So I thought.

No matter who I decided to apply for a car loan with, I needed to lift the security freeze on my credit files. I purposely kept my files frozen to ensure my information was protected and to prohibit me from applying for credit unnecessarily. After I lifted the security freeze on all three credit files, I went to sleep. When I woke up the next morning, I was nervous but hopeful. I knew I had to apply for an auto loan, but I was unsure who I would apply with. After only a few minutes of thinking about it, I applied with Navy Federal Credit Union. I figured the worse that could happen was I would receive another rejection. Little did I realize, God was already working things out on my behalf.

When I decided to apply with Navy Federal, I was nervous, but I did not stress long. I went to the email offer they previously sent and clicked on the "apply now" link. The link took me to the Navy Federal log-in page. When I logged in with my credentials, my personal information was prepopulated. It was a pretty straight forward and short application. Since I did not want a car over $20K, I applied for a $20K loan. This included a downpayment of

$2K, which resulted in a loan amount for $18K. The offer Navy Federal sent me via email included interest rates that ranged from 4.5 percent -18.8 percent. Any rate under 20 percent was a win for me. I filled out all the remaining questions and clicked submit.

Within 3-5 seconds, I received an instant pre-approval. I literally cried tears of joy. Not only did I receive an instant approval, but the interest rates I was eligible for were pretty low. If I purchased a new car and financed for six years, the interest rate would be 5.99 percent. If I purchased a late model used car and financed for six years, the interest rate would be 7.79 percent. Considering my current interest rate was over 15 percent, I was overwhelmed with joy! Once I received my pre-approval, I printed my confirmation page and thanked God over and over again. I was crying real tears because I was not expecting such an amazing blessing. Little did I know, God was not finished.

I took a shower, got dressed, and drove to Progressive service center to signed the required paperwork. Once I signed the power of attorney, my part was complete. I was waiting for my lien holder to sign their document so Progressive could release my payment. When I finished at Progressive service center, I drove to a

Navy Federal branch to pick up the check to purchase my car. It was such a seamless process. When I arrived, I told the banker I was pre-approved for an auto loan, and I came in to pick up the check. She verified my ID, pulled up my account, walked to the office, and came back with the check. I was still in denial that this was really happening. She explained what I needed to do to ensure the dealership got paid. After she provided those details, she told me what I needed to do to ensure the title was sent directly to Navy Federal. Everything was seamless. All I needed to do was find a car.

After I left Navy Federal, I went to the chiropractor office for my scheduled treatment. Since I had not seen my parents since the car accident on July 3rd, I decided to drive to their home and give them an update. As I imagined, my parents were grateful and happy to see me. I shared with my dad the news about the pre-approval and picking up the check to pay for the car. He was filled with joy to know that things were working out well for me. While I was at my parents' home, my claims representative reached out to let me know all required paperwork had been received.

Wow, things were moving pretty quickly! I was in disbelief. Then again, I knew the God I served was real, and He always made a way, even when I did not see a way. My claims representative admitted never having a case that moved so quickly through this process. I told her that I was not her typical client. Since all the paperwork was received, that meant she could release the payment.

Within an hour, I received the link to accept the payment electronically. After I verified my claim number and zip code, I gained access to the link. I entered my debit card information, and the payment for $7,492.43 was posted to my account instantly. I was once again overwhelmed with joy. God was continuously showing out on my behalf. While I was still at my parents' home, I discovered that Sam's Club had a Car Buyer Program. If an individual purchased a vehicle from a TrueCar dealership, they could receive a gift card for $110. Every incentive counted so I wanted to capitalize on any offers provided to me.

When I got home, I started looking for reasonable cars to purchase. By going through the Sam's Club Car Buyer Program, each time I clicked on a dealership, an inquiry was sent to the dealership. That resulted in lots of calls, texts and emails. I was on the phone with sales associates for hours. It was overwhelming. Every time I found a car that was in my budget, I was told to receive the price listed online, I could not have outside financing. That was the case with almost every dealership I spoke with.

I could not believe no one was willing to accept my outside financing without increasing the cost of the car. I was concerned. I received an email from Hyundai of McDonough introducing another sales associate. I was tired of spending time on the phone, sending texts and emails. I shared with him what I was looking for, how much I could put down on a car, and the outside financing that I already had from Navy Federal. I explained that if they were not willing to work with me, I did not want to spend time going back and forth. After I sent my email, I did not get a response, so I moved forward. After numerous encounters with sales associates indicating I had to finance through the dealership to get the lower price, I was drained.

Instead of spending time on the phone, I located potential cars that I could fit in my budget. There were three cars that I located on Hyundai of McDonough website. Since I had not heard back from the individual who emailed me, I called the dealership. A receptionist answered the phone and was very professional and personable. I shared with her that I found three cars online that I was interested in purchasing, but I already had outside financing. I asked if they would be willing to let me purchase the car at the price listed online. Since she was not a sales associate, she told me she needed to speak with her general manager, so she asked if she could put me on hold. After holding for a few minutes, she came back to the line. She told me that usually to receive discounts, incentives, or the lowest price on a car, it had to be financed through the dealership. However, the general manager told her that if I come in to purchase a car, they would honor the price I saw online.

I was hopeful. I asked her to provide me with her name and the general manager's name so I would know who to ask for when I arrived the next day. As soon as I ended the call, I received a response from the sales associate who reached out to me previously. He shared with me he was willing to do whatever he could to help close the deal. That was what I needed to hear. When I arrived at the dealership on Friday, July 9th, I received a warm welcome from the sales associate, and we got down to business. I reiterated again what I was looking for and how much I was willing to pay. He understood and respected my needs. He wanted to know if I had any flexibility, and I explained it would ultimately depend on what was offered.

After some time had passed, the sales associate came and got me so we could test drive some cars. I was optimistic that we would get the deal done. When we walked outside, he handed me the keys and pointed to the car we would be driving. Before we got to the car, I asked the year of the car because it looked new. He told me the car was a 2024 model. I was surprised. I asked him if he was serious or playing with my emotions. He reassured me he was very serious, and this was one of the cars they were working to put me in. He told me if I liked the car and could put at least $4K down, they could close the deal for me. I was in awe of the goodness of God. When I got in the car, it only had 10 miles. It was very nice, spacious, and exceeded my expectations. It drove really well, too. After the test drive, I was sold. I was ready to sign on the dotted line. I was so happy. Before we walked back inside, I asked if this model had a remote start option. He told me it did, and if a specific car did not have it, I could add an aftermarket option at a later time. Though I was not interested in any aftermarket options, I was interested in exploring a car with a remote start option. When we walked back inside the dealership, I waited for the managers to prepare the paperwork. During that time, I took a moment to thank God for being so good to me. I was so blessed.

It took more time than I expected to get the paperwork from the managers, but I waited patiently. After some time passed, my sales associate asked me to step outside with him again. When I did, he pushed the remote he was holding in his hand, and it started a second car that was parked next to the car we test drove. I was so excited! I said to the sales associate, "You found a car that has a remote start!" He said to me, "What if I told you I could offer you this car with more features for the same price?" I could not believe it. I was in denial. He reassured me there was no catch. The only difference was there were more miles on the car since it was a demo car for one of the managers. Even though the car had more miles than the first car, it was still considered a new car according to Navy Federal guidelines. That also meant instead of a 7.79 percent interest rate, the interest rate would only be 5.99 percent. I was winning!

When the deal was done, I purchased a 2024 Hyundai Elantra SEL for only $22K. My monthly payments with Navy Federal, which included GAP insurance, would only be $306. This was my newest car and the payment was lower than my previous car. I got the deal done by myself. I was ecstatic! I named my new car White Diamond 2.0. From May 2024 through July 2024, I endured many obstacles. I encountered several challenges, ups, and downs. Through it all, God was faithful. Every situation that God brought me to, He brought me through. I was wrongly released from a job after 10 years of service, but I overcame. I was involved in a bad car accident that could have claimed my life, but God spared me. Through pain, anxiety, frustrations and stress, I overcame. I am an overcomer. I know as long as I have God on my side, I will make it. I know as long as I have a praying family, I can make it. I know as long as I have supportive, authentic and transparent sistas in my circle, I know I can take whatever obstacles come my way. I am an OVERCOMER!

CHAPTER 7 SUMMARY

It is true in most cases God gives his toughest assignments to his strongest children. In my 43 years of living, I have endured so much. However, God has been good to me no matter the situation. It is so easy to give up when things are going wrong, but I encourage you to keep going, keep fighting, and never give up. I know things get hard sometimes, but God will always make a way. God will watch over us. He will keep us. He will show up and show out when we least expect it. It is so true that we must not grow weary in well doing for in due season we will reap if we faint not. Remember, God will never leave you nor forsake you. Keep believing and have faith.

ACKNOWLEDGMENTS

Father God, I thank you once again for leading and guiding me on this journey for the third time. I am forever grateful. I know sometimes I am not worthy, but you still love me. Thank you for giving me the words to say. I cannot thank you enough.

To the love of my heart, I did it again! Thank you for being on this journey through life with me. I could not imagine this life without you in it. I love you.

Lisa King DeJesus, we did it again, sis, x3! Thank you so much for being supportive and encouraging. I truly could not do this without you. My words will never be enough to convey just how much I appreciate you. Thank you for your patience with me. I know it is not always easy, but I mean well! Forever grateful for you.

OBEDIENCE

AUTHOR BIOGRAPHY

An Atlanta native, Sheirra Marci is an inspiring, authentic, and enthusiastic author sharing her life experiences to help educate, motivate and heal her audience. Her passion for writing has fueled this desire to share the meaningful blessings she has encountered, in addition to the powerful life lessons she has learned. After publishing her second book, "Resilience: A Moment to Reflect, Restore, and Renew" in 2024, Sheirra Marci discovered that her story continued to uplift, inspire and encourage her audience. The positive feedback made her eager to give individuals more. The third installment of her memoir series was not what she planned. However, she needed to be obedient to God's word. Therefore, "Obedience: A Season to Observe, Obey, & Overcome" was born.

Since obtaining her Doctor of Education degree, Sheirra Marci has focused on offering high-quality educational services through her business, Dr. Marci Nspirations Group LLC. She provides in-person and virtual tutoring services. Her focus areas are English, writing, spelling, basic math up to 9th grade, and standardized test preparation. As she approaches 13 years in business, she continues to be highly rated on Google.

In addition to her tutoring business, Sheirra Marci runs a thriving sisterhood organization. Dedicated to empowering and encouraging like-minded women on purpose, she birthed the SIS Selebrating in Sisterhood Organization in December 2023. As the organization approaches two years old, Sheirra Marci is committed to building a powerful network of women who embody support, service and sisterhood. The organization also offers a program for girls aged 12-25, the LSIS S2S Mentorship Program.

Sheirra Marci is grateful for all the opportunities God has provided over the last few years. She continues to share each moment with her family, friends, King, students, parents, Sista circle, and the SIS organization. We only have one chance to live this thing called life, and she wants to leave an impactful stamp on the world while she can.

www.ingramcontent.com/pod-product-compliance
Lightning Source LLC
Chambersburg PA
CBHW070915130626
46555CB00001B/140